"In *Overcoming Imposter Anxiety*, Ijeoma Nwaogu offers the quintessential guide to overcoming imposter anxiety. She offers a joyful strategy to master the inner critic and become the best version of ourselves with this easy-to-follow guide where she includes charts, case examples, and questions that challenge and realign our perspectives. Nwaogu wrote a road map to walking the walk, confidently and calm with your head held high."

—**Kim Lee Hughes, PhD**, past president and archivist of the
Association of Multicultural Counseling & Development

"Ijeoma Nwaogu diligently introduces the concept of imposter anxiety, a phenomenon that impacts people from all walks of life. With relatable examples, reassurance, and honesty, Ijeoma presents the multidimensional elements of imposter anxiety, which goes a long way in dispelling a one-size-fits-all approach to dealing with this phenomenon. Do not expect quick fixes in this book. The tools that Ijeoma provides require honest conversations, deliberate practice, and frequent reflection."

—**Nyasha M. GuramatunhuCooper, PhD**
leadership educator, facilitator, speaker, a
Girton Road Leadership Learning and Co

"I recommend *Overcoming Imposter Anxiety* because without managing imposter anxiety, you will have a difficult time setting and achieving goals. This book gives empowerment, tips, and insights to help readers reduce imposter anxiety. The check-ins throughout the book promote thoughtful reflection that will allow readers to reflect and process feelings."

—**Latasha Matthews**, licensed professional counselor; "America's
Emotional Wellness Expert;" and CEO and clinical director of
Illumination Counseling and Coaching, and Why 2 Live Well

"Ijeoma Nwaogu has included her vast personal and professional experiences to provide readers with practical and very useful strategies for overcoming imposter anxiety. This very helpful book is easy to read, and the personal stories made it very relatable. I also found the check-ins throughout the book very helpful. This book is a must-read for anyone dealing with imposter anxiety!"

—**Rosell Jenkins**, licensed psychologist; author of *Cultivating Joy*;
and owner of Mental Wellness Services, PC

"Ijeoma Nwaogu applies a very personable approach to a common phenomenon experienced by many new and transitioning professionals. She presents a much-needed, refreshing undertaking that dissects the intricacies of imposter anxiety in a manner that is relatable and professional. The book lives up to its title as it is designed to incite internal dialogue and reflection on ways for overcoming imposter anxiety."

> —**Anissa Howard, PhD, LPC, LMFT, RPT-S, ACS, NCC, CAADC,** assistant professor and program coordinator of clinical mental health counseling at Fort Valley State University

"Some of the most famous people in our time have experienced imposter anxiety at some point in their lives, but without understanding the origins of this feeling. *Overcoming Imposter Anxiety* is a deeply authentic narrative with practical underpinnings of how to recognize, cope, and move beyond imposter anxiety without experiencing shame and guilt. This wonderful read for growth fostering self-actualization proves that self-acceptance is possible."

> —**Nathaniel Brown, PhD,** lecturer of clinical mental health counseling, and clinical director in the counseling program at the Johns Hopkins University School of Education

"Ijeoma Nwaogu's work and expertise on conquering imposter anxiety is extremely timely and highly needed in all settings. Imposter anxiety is a topic we have all experienced at some point in our personal and professional lives, and she has done an exceptional job in providing actionable and practical steps to help individuals identify how imposter anxiety impacts their daily lives and ways they can conquer it in order to thrive."

> —**Chinasa Elue, PhD,** associate professor of educational leadership and higher education at Kennesaw State University

OVERCOMING IMPOSTER ANXIETY

MOVE BEYOND FEAR *of* FAILURE *and* SELF-DOUBT *to* EMBRACE YOUR WORTHY, CAPABLE SELF

Ijeoma C. Nwaogu, PhD

New Harbinger Publications, Inc.

Publisher's Note

This publication is designed to provide accurate and authoritative information in regard to the subject matter covered. It is sold with the understanding that the publisher is not engaged in rendering psychological, financial, legal, or other professional services. If expert assistance or counseling is needed, the services of a competent professional should be sought.

NEW HARBINGER PUBLICATIONS is a registered trademark of New Harbinger Publications, Inc.

New Harbinger Publications is an employee-owned company.

Copyright © 2023 by Ijeoma C. Nwaogu
New Harbinger Publications, Inc.
5720 Shattuck Avenue
Oakland, CA 94609
www.newharbinger.com

Cover design by Sara Christian

Acquired by Georgia Kolias

Edited by Brady Kahn

Library of Congress Cataloging-in-Publication Data on file

Printed in the United States of America

25   24   23

10   9   8   7   6   5   4   3   2   1   First Printing

Your worth and capacity
cannot be gauged
nor can they be limited
by any metric,
any norm,
or anyone's expectations.
You are worthy and capable beyond measure.
Your potential is without bounds.
Will you give yourself permission
to tap into your infinite greatness?

Contents

Introduction

We can do hard things. We can overcome challenging circumstances. We can surmount our fears. I learned this after I was involved in a car crash when I was twenty-two. It was a hit-and-run, to be exact. Someone in a yellow sportscar slammed into the back of my vehicle, then disappeared into the night. Round and round, my car spun three times on the seven-lane expressway. You hear the common saying, "My life flashed before my eyes." Well, I experienced this firsthand. The positive memories and heartfelt milestones in my life came to mind in just a few seconds, like an old movie reel. That night, I realized how powerful the human brain is. While these rushing recollections flickered through my thoughts, I was ferociously turning my steering wheel. I had no idea if I was going to collide into oncoming cars or if I was spiraling toward other vehicles in front of me. I thought, *So this is how my life ends.* But seconds in, somehow, my car stopped spinning. The smoke cleared. And I ended up with my car facing the forward-moving direction. I spotted the yellow sportscar speeding off. The driver entered the nearest exit and fled the scene. No cars were coming, but I needed to get out of the way. So, with haste, I collected myself, watchfully drove off onto the side of the highway, then called for help. The back of my car was demolished. Luckily, I wasn't severely harmed, but I had to visit my neurologist, and then receive chiropractic treatments multiple times a week for two years.

After the weekend of the crash, I had to head back to campus for graduate classes. My mother brought a rental car to the house, so I could use it to return to school. With my mom by my side, I loaded the trunk, then approached the driver side door. I froze. It was as if I'd seen a snake slithering on the steering wheel. I couldn't get in. Panic had overtaken me, and I burst into a deep sob. I felt powerless. Filled with fright, I whispered in a trembling voice, "I can't do this." My mom leaned in to console me while offering words of encouragement. A couple of minutes later, I gathered myself as much as I could. Then finally, I got in. I slowly sat in the driver's seat and buckled my belt. "Bye, Mommy," I uttered in a small, reluctant tone. Then, I took a deep breath and, with immense caution, began my hour-and-a-half-long journey back to school.

I mark this car crash as one of the hardest and scariest experiences I've ever gone through. Driving again just two days after the incident was tough. But in my reflection of the incident, I gained an important takeaway: we face difficult situations, like car accidents or other run-ins that leave us feeling afraid and helpless, but despite these instances, *we are capable of overcoming them.* The hit-and-run was out of my control. But what was *in* my control was how I responded after the event. I had a choice: I could either succumb to the fear or surmount it.

I remember this wisdom now when I face all sorts of challenging situations, and I want to offer it to you as you embark on your journey to overcome imposter anxiety. You can let fear get in your way, especially when you experience the anxiety of self-doubt. You know the feeling. I'm talking about those moments when you feel inadequate, unworthy, incompetent, undeserving, or inferior. Because you fear failure or being exposed as a fraud, you become discouraged from moving toward promising paths in your life.

After that hit-and-run, I never wanted to enter another automobile again. But I can imagine what divorcing from driving would have cost me. I had places to go, people to see, things to do, and aspirations to actualize. I was terrified of driving again, sure. *But I needed to do it anyway.* This turned out to be a powerful lesson as I contended with crushing anxiety as a grad student. For two years, I toiled with the most overwhelming feelings of self-doubt I'd ever endure. By sharing the moments when imposter anxiety has hit me the hardest, my hope is that you'll recognize enough of your experience to know this book can help.

When Imposter Anxiety Hit Me Hard

I vividly recall one afternoon when I returned to my apartment after class. Like a dead man walking, I paced over to my bed and plopped on it. I hated that mattress. It was so uncomfortable. But I lay there, glaring at the ceiling, as the embarrassing recollections of my silence in class replayed over and over in my mind. I was so scared to speak in class that I barely uttered a word. I was one of the fifteen students who were admitted into a program ranked among the top three in the nation. In my cohort were peers who came with a wealth of knowledge and lived experiences—all of which I thought were superior to my own. Despite my previous accomplishments in college—making good grades, achieving wild success as a student leader, and gaining acceptance into a reputable master's program—I still felt completely out of place. I frequently thought, *What on earth am I doing here?* I didn't think I had the smarts and know-how to demonstrate my value. I assumed, *They probably chose me to meet a diversity quota, not because I deserve it.*

Carrying this load of shame, I tussled through the same routine ordeal for each course I took. It went something like this: I enter class. The professor delivers her discourse. She invites her students to share thoughts on a topic. My classmates shoot their hands in the air. Most of them offer their reflections. Then my internal battle begins. The pressure intensifies with each passing hour. Everyone has spoken except me. I want to share my perspectives, but the hand of fear holds my mouth shut. *Will my classmates side-eye my opinions? Am I just taking up space in this highly coveted program?* I had it drilled into my head that my ideas lacked substance. So I keep quiet.

Why couldn't I just raise my hand to voice my views? All the while I refrained from talking, it was to "protect" myself from appearing as a phony. But in my mind, my silence still exposed me as such. It was like a catch-22—damned if I did and damned if I didn't. I wanted to break away from this vicious cycle. So, once in a while, I'd set expectations for myself the night before each class. My plan was to raise my hand to share my ideas at least once: *I can do this. There's nothing to fear. I've got this.* Achieving this single objective required plenty of positive self-talk to muster up enough courage to make just one quick remark. To my surprise, I met my goal for a day or two, but it was short-lived. I reverted to my mute state, and it became my daily ritual. The negative thoughts in my head relentlessly dissuaded me from participating in class. I badly needed the work in the book you're now reading: to unlearn self-limiting notions and adopt empowering truths about my identity. But at the time, I wasn't aware of how to do it. So I ended up repeating the awful sequence of showing up, speechless and uncomfortable as ever, for all my three-hour-long classes.

Now I'm not shy. I like to express myself. I appreciated my graduate school experience. So why in the world did I feel like a complete fraud? As time progressed, I grew more and more curious about this question. I began exploring a few factors, and here's what I discovered. There were several triggers that sparked my reaction, like my environment, the kind of support I had, and internalized beliefs. The classroom format was new for me. The environment was competitive. And the pressure to meet high expectations was a factor. My classmates were supportive, for the most part. But a more invested approach from those holding power in those spaces—like my professors—could have gone a long way to empower me. I also felt outnumbered as one of the few people of color. And much of the views about my adequacy and belonging were shaped by false narratives I had subconsciously assumed over time. I had absorbed inaccurate messages about who I was and what I deserved. And my skepticism about my capabilities was a cloak, concealing the person I desired to be in that setting.

These triggers altogether affected how I moved through my master's program, like the times I withheld useful insights my classmates could have learned from. You too could be provoked by multiple forces—some in your control and some outside it. But just as I learned how to overcome my triggers, you can do the same. You can become privy to the strategies for moving beyond fear and self-doubt to fully embrace your worthy, capable self.

Why I Wrote This Book

As I discovered how to work with different triggers, I awakened to the fact that many people struggle with the same sort of experience. This is true, no matter the situation, whether this fear strikes at school, work, home, or in social circles or when it comes to wellness, finances, and relationships. I started working with talented individuals who struggled with seeing themselves as *enough*. The problem with feeling inadequate is that you end up sabotaging your pursuits when, in fact, you are enough and hold enormous potential to thrive. As someone who is passionate about the personal success of others, I began seeking ways to help others, from all sorts of backgrounds, to move past fear and self-doubt to live the lives they crave. I started speaking at conferences on the topic. I created trainings about it for various universities I worked for. And later, I began flirting with the idea of writing a book. That intention fell into a coma once I entered the rat race of life. But one event in particular resuscitated this idea.

It's time to get to typing: this realization came to me as I gazed over at what looked like the longest after-session crowd. I had just finished giving a talk to incoming MBA students at Rice University, where attendees who wanted to connect with me waited afterward, forming an extensive single-file line.

"I just wanted to tell you, this was so helpful! Thank you so much," most of them professed as they reached for a handshake or a hug. Several shared their stories with me, and some fished for feedback to address their own dealings with self-doubt. The eye-opener for me was not just the visual of the lengthy line of people anticipating a chance to express their appreciation but also the outpouring of heartfelt narratives and solution-seeking inquiries. Writing this book could no longer remain just an idea. It had to become a reality. *I must move forward with it*, I knew.

But despite this knowing, I danced with my own doubts about this project. I am not a psychologist. I am simply a student of life with an appetite for understanding the experience of fear and self-doubt. My commitment to helping people overcome this reaction also stems from my vision of the world. I imagine a life where we all live out our biggest ambitions and pursue our infinite potential. But to lean into this dream, we need the proper ingredients to get there: self-efficacy and a sense of self-worth. With the solution for moving toward my vision in my toolbox, I began the process.

Creating this book involved pulling from my own experiences with imposter anxiety. I also included recommended solutions from psychology research and other scholarly works on the topic. I recognize, though, powerful insights about fear and self-doubt are also inspired by those outside of mental health professions. This includes former first lady Michelle Obama, who recounted her experience with imposter anxiety during her 2018 talk at the Anderson School in London: "I had to work to overcome that question that I always ask myself: Am I good enough? That's a question that has dogged me for a good part of my life" (Obama 2018). Despite this thought, Mrs. Obama pushed through, accomplishing so much over the years and continuously inspiring the masses with her story.

My friend Emma is another reference on the topic. "I don't know if I'm 'expert' enough," she said. Initially, Emma was nervous about starting a YouTube channel. But she pressed on anyway, sidestepping her self-doubt, and establishing her very own show on the platform. Famous or not, a person's experience with overcoming imposter anxiety holds transformative power. It was, therefore, important for me to include personal accounts of individuals from various walks of life, because it reveals a common link connecting us all: our experiences with fear and self-doubt.

Who Am I?

People have all sorts of perspectives when it comes to overcoming self-doubt. But this book will highlight my own. It was through my lens that this resource was written. So, it's important to know who I am. My identity, personal accounts, and worldviews shaped the contents and the approach of this book. So, here's what to know about me.

I am a Black woman living in an upper-income, suburban household in Houston, Texas. I was born in Lagos, Nigeria, and immigrated to the United

States at age four. I grew up in New York City and Augusta, Georgia in a two-parent, middle-income household. Having schooled, worked, and lived in Atlanta, Georgia between the ages of seventeen and thirty-one, and with the culture imbedded in me, I consider this city a hometown. I am the daughter of two highly educated parents, a middle child with five siblings, and am the mother of three children under the age of thirteen. I consider myself open-minded, structured, self-aware, and intuitive. And I'm an extroverted introvert.

I'm a credentialed leadership coach, holding a bachelor's degree in psychology and sociology, a master's degree in college student affairs administration, and a doctorate in counseling. I'm a product of public schooling, from first grade to my terminal degree. And I've been an educator and administrator in both public and private higher education settings. After about eight years as an employee, I felt called to entrepreneurship and to helping clients achieve their life, leadership, career, and business goals. I do so in a variety of ways, including speaking and coaching. I have a keen interest in social psychology, and I enjoy creating and providing resources for personal development.

I have experienced maltreatment in the forms of xenophobia, racism, sexism, colorism, ageism, adultism, and classism—and I'm an ongoing overcomer of these imposter anxiety-triggering forms of oppression. I also recognize my unearned privileges as nondisabled, straight, Christian, married, and a United States citizen. I am committed to lifelong learning and educating myself about the lives of others to build my empathy. On an ongoing basis, I work to decondition my mind from self-limiting notions, so I can fill it with positive truths about who I am. I'm opposed to oppressive structures in all of their forms. And I believe people are gifted and whole. My guiding values are diversity, freedom, authenticity, compassion, wisdom, purpose, and love. I wrote this book during the latter part of the COVID-19 pandemic, a time when a global prevalence of anxiety was increased (World Health Organization 2022), and the world was undergoing a major shift in the way we think about and pursue life (Wang 2020).

Theoretical Approaches

Because of who I am and what I believe, a couple of theoretical frameworks were important and appropriate for me to use as guides for producing this book: these are the philosophies of liberation psychology and cognitive behavioral therapy (CBT). In exploring the root of imposter anxiety, I recognized external factors, like oppressive social environments, as being primary contributors of the experience. Traditional psychology often fails to acknowledge the role of these factors, but this book won't. Much of the sentiment around "imposter syndrome" tends to point the finger at those experiencing it without calling out toxic and abusive spaces and structures this reaction is sparked by. To address this, I've incorporated liberation psychology, which points out the influences of systems of social oppression (Goodman 2015).

Liberation psychology has two broad aims: healing and freedom. One of my goals in this book is to help you identify unhealed emotional wounds that produce imposter anxiety. These include harms that were inflicted upon you from oppressive environments. By identifying these contributing factors and doing the work to overcome imposter anxiety, you can experience greater freedom, and therefore, a chance to lean into your authentic self. Liberation psychology also integrates storytelling, challenges the status quo, and advocates for disconnecting from self-limiting beliefs. Receiving and giving support are also part of liberation psychology. And the approach acknowledges both nature and nurture factors of your experiences with self-doubt. It encourages self-compassion and rest to counter anxiety-provoking ways of being, like perfectionism and hustle culture. It recognizes all people as capable and worthy. And it supports the reclaiming of personal power and the pursuit of a boundless life.

Liberation psychology also encompasses cognitive behavioral methods, which I'll use to suggest mind-shift insights and action steps for overcoming imposter anxiety. CBT emphasizes how your thoughts shape your feelings and actions. For example, if you *think* you are incompetent, you may react with *feelings* of fear or anxiety. This can lead to *behaviors* like silence or avoidance of certain situations. But if you believe you're capable, you may respond with curiosity or eagerness. You approach your goals instead of avoiding them. So an aim of CBT is to reframe your thoughts and feelings to ultimately change your behavior. This way, you can reduce your self-doubts and do the things you desire.

What You'll Learn

This book is your ultimate guide for understanding and addressing fear and self-doubt. I've included answers to frequently asked questions I've collected on the topic during my guest appearances on podcasts, coaching sessions, and speaking engagements. In this book, the following questions will be answered, as you may be curious about them, too:

Is this an experience I'm really having?

Can I be a confident person and still deal with imposter anxiety?

Does my identity have anything to do with it?

Are my feelings of inadequacy my fault?

Is self-doubt a sign of humility?

What will happen if I don't address it?

Will I ever get over this reaction?

You'll learn the ins and outs of imposter anxiety—who it affects, what it looks like, and where, when, and why it happens. You'll see how your biology and your environment influence the experience. You'll understand how factors like competition, perceived worthiness, fear of failure, past traumatic events, perceived differences, ego, and your levels of support prompt this reaction. You'll also learn of the surprising gifts of self-doubt. Most importantly, you'll build an overcomer's mindset and gain transformative strategies to navigate the experience in the best ways possible. You'll find places to check in with yourself throughout the chapters, and I encourage you to keep a journal as you go through these parts. Writing down your reflections allows you to think deeply about your responses to the prompts. This way, you make the most of your reading experience and you remain invested in doing the work to move beyond imposter anxiety. You'll also find some free tools available at http://www.newharbinger.com/51086.

How This Book Will Benefit You

I had to overcome imposter anxiety to remain the course in fulfilling many of my life goals and activities, like speaking up in my doctoral program, becoming an entrepreneur, and initiating contact with my book publisher. Since you're reading this book, it tells me you want to go after your dreams, too. I urge you to do so, because here's what could happen if you don't:

Toxic beliefs can guide you, and you leave room for past hurts to rule your actions. You risk feeling powerless, unworthy, undeserving, and incapable. You could operate under the assumption that your difference is a disadvantage. You gamble with feeling insecure, isolated, and insufficient, with unmitigated imposter anxiety leading you down a path of misery and regret.

But when you use the tools provided in this book, here's what you can look forward to: Expect to raise your hand more, speak up more, and take charge of your life. You get to revive your personal agency. You'll expand yourself, occupy space, embrace your unique qualities, and live more courageously and authentically. You'll know you are worthy, belonging, deserving, and capable. You'll feel optimistic, assured, and more comfortable in your own skin. And you get to fulfill your potential and pursue your biggest aspirations, while doing your part to change the world for the better. You can redirect the trajectory of your life in all these ways, and more. So, consider this question: how would you be different if fear and self-doubt weren't factors in your life?

I wish I had a book like this early on in grad school. It would have been the saving grace I needed to step into my highest and truest self during that cherished period of my life. You are in for a real, life-changing treat when you apply the information from this book. The knowledge I'll share with you helped me triumph over my own self-doubts over time. It's also equipped many clients from different walks of life to move past similar challenges. As you progress along this journey, I urge you to use your newfound awareness to help others see their own value and believe in their capacity to live their desired life. The opportunity to overcome imposter anxiety is ahead. If you're ready, I've got your hand. Let's jump right in.

CHAPTER 1

An Experience of Fear and Self-Doubt

Four out of five. The number of people who deal with "imposter syndrome" can reach this astounding rate, with up to 82 percent of all people experiencing this reaction at some point in their lives (Bravata et al. 2020). But for this predicament to be so prevalent in the daily walks of so many, what is it exactly? And where in the world did it come from?

Self-doubt has existed for as long as humans have. And for multiple millennia, we've met fear in all its forms, including the fear of being outed as a fraud. However, 1978 was the year when words were given to this reaction. Two clinical psychologists, Dr. Pauline Clance and Dr. Suzanne Imes, coined the phrase "impostor phenomenon" (1978). I am reminded of LL Cool J's unforgettable chant, "Something Like a Phenomenon," from his 1997 Billboard-topping hit. In the song, he raps about his rendezvous with a lady friend, naming it a phenomenon. In this book, however, I'll guide you in exploring your own rendezvous, though not as sexy, with a different phenomenon—the imposter phenomenon.

What names have you heard people use to describe this experience? Maybe you've heard folks call it an inferiority complex, self-sabotage, or the inner critic. The more familiar expression, though, is imposter syndrome. But let's take a moment to inspect the words "imposter" and "syndrome."

One thing we know about this phenomenon is that it's experienced by highly capable individuals who hold enormous potential. They are nowhere near frauds. So, using the word "imposter" isn't intended to imply that you're an imposter if you're dealing with self-doubt. Instead, it's included to describe how people have *felt* when navigating this experience.

Look at the word "syndrome" as well. It's been long used to label pathological conditions and diagnosable ailments. A syndrome signifies an abnormality. Imposter phenomenon, however, is far from abnormal. It's not a mental disorder. Instead, it's a common lived experience shared by many of us. These are the very reasons I don't use of the word "syndrome" to discuss this experience. So, to refine our understanding of this phenomenon, and to describe it more explicitly, I offer a slightly new naming of it. The American Psychological Association describes anxiety as being made up of worried thoughts and emotional tension, like thinking you're inadequate or feeling unsafe. Because the imposter phenomenon fits under the umbrella of anxiety, I refer to the experience of fear and self-doubt as *imposter anxiety*.

What Is Imposter Anxiety?

Some people have diagnosable anxiety disorders when their levels of anxiety are disproportionate to the trigger. But this is not the type of anxiety I am referring to in this book. I am talking about imposter anxiety as a normal, appropriate reaction to life's challenging situations. With imposter anxiety, your reaction is proportionate to the conditions you're facing. Anxiety disorders, however, come up for oftentimes unknown reasons and last for long periods of time even after leaving a triggering situation (Canadian Mental Health Association, BC Division 2015).

Imposter anxiety and anxiety disorders share some similarities in how they are experienced. But here's how imposter anxiety is different: it happens because of specific triggers and lasts only if those circumstances exist. Some anxiety disorders may feel impossible to manage without medication, but imposter anxiety doesn't require such measures. I'll give you the tools you need to move past this experience in the most effective ways possible.

Who Experiences Imposter Anxiety?

Most people will face imposter anxiety at different junctures throughout their lives (Ahlfeld 2009). So, you've likely dealt with it at some point along your journey—just like any other person—including folks we hold in the highest esteem and whose achievements are easy to recognize. Take Meta Platforms' former chief operating officer Sheryl Sandberg, as an example. In her book, *Lean In: Women, Work, and the Will to Lead*, Sandberg wrote: "Every time I was called on in class, I was sure that I was about to embarrass myself. Every time I took a test, I was sure that it had gone badly. And every time I didn't embarrass myself—or even excelled—I believed that I had fooled everyone yet again. One day soon, the jig would be up" (Sandberg and Scovell 2013). During an interview on NPR's Fresh Air in 2016, Tom Hanks—who has won numerous accolades throughout his career, including two Oscars, seven Primetime Emmys, and four Golden Globe Awards—said, "There comes a point where you think how did I get here and am I going to be able to continue this? When are they going to discover that I am, in fact, a fraud and take everything away from me?" Another example is Viola Davis, author of the memoir *Finding Me* and first Black actor to achieve the Triple Crown of Acting. During a 2017 interview with ABC News, she said, "It feels like my hard work has paid off, but at the same time I still have the impostor…syndrome. I still feel like…I'm going to wake up and everybody's going to see me for the hack I am." Lastly, look at Jennifer Lopez, a wildly sought-after singer and actress, who revealed, "Even though I had sold 70 million records, there I was feeling like, I'm not good at this" (Dunn 2013).

Learning about decorated public figures' experiences with self-doubt illuminates how widespread this phenomenon is. Although the original research on imposter phenomenon studied primarily White women in their twenties, thirties, and forties, you can face imposter anxiety, no matter your demographic, personality, status, role, or upbringing (Caselman, Self, and Self 2006). It can show up when you're involved in all sorts of life activities, big and small. Can you imagine the multitude of situations where imposter anxiety unfolds?

As a student, you're preoccupied with the question *Am I intelligent enough?* High school was a breeze for you. Then you enter university. Your studies stretch you beyond what you could have ever imagined. Your grades suffer. You start to believe, *I don't have what it takes to survive this place.*

With dating, the question in your mind is, *Am I charming enough?* You finally go on a date with the hot guy you've been eyeing for some time now. He compliments you on your humor, but a sharp wave goes through your stomach when you think, *It's only a matter of time before he realizes I'm not that interesting.*

In peer circles, you fear, *Am I cool enough?* You're trying to make new friends. And your concern is *Will they like me? Do I have the right personality for them?*

With your family, you speculate, *Am I sane enough?* Each time you visit home for the holidays, you get into a big argument with your relatives. Their judgmental comments offend you. So you snap back at them before storming off. You feel misunderstood, and you fear they'll think you're mentally unstable.

As a religious person, you question, *Am I holy enough?* You notice how your faith-filled peers read their daily devotionals. They don't miss a single day. And Bible quotes flow out of their mouths like water. You, on the other hand, find it difficult to keep up with the Good Book consistently. You barely remember verses from it, and you feel unworthy when you're around others who seem more disciplined about their faith than you.

As a professional, you contemplate, *Am I skilled enough?* Your boss offers you a promotion. But you immediately assume, *Gosh, I bamboozled him into believing I can do this job.*

As a spouse, you worry, *Am I sexy enough?* You've been married for several years. You're getting older and your body is changing. You become more conscious about your physical appearance, *What if he realizes I'm not as attractive as I used to be?*

As a parent, you wonder, *Am I good enough?* You bring your newborn home from the hospital. You need to take care of yourself after giving birth, but you feel pressured to quickly bounce back and do everything perfectly to get your home together and your baby settled. Mom guilt sets in.

Regarding your physical wellness, your concern is, *Am I fit enough?* You haven't exercised in a while, and you feel like a slob. You want to go to the gym, but you avoid it. You're self-conscious about exposing your "unfit" body.

As a multiethnic person, you consider, *Am I similar enough?* You think you're a "watered down" version of your Japanese and Dominican identities. When you visit your Japanese side of your family, you stand out. You don't look like them. And when you're around your Dominican family, your way of speaking is as distinct as a full moon in the sky. You don't sound like them. So, you feel stuck in the murky middle. You're not sure where you belong.

As a leader, your fear is, *Is my level of social awareness enough?* After giving a talk, you get questions from the audience about racism. You're wary of making offensive remarks. So you tread carefully in your speech and end up stumbling over your words.

CHECKING IN   You can see how imposter anxiety shows up in all kinds of situations. Which of the scenarios can you relate to the most?

When Does Imposter Anxiety Happen?

Imposter anxiety surfaces when you're facing new or challenging situations. It can happen before, during, and after an activity (Lane 2015). To understand this better, follow this story path to see how imposter anxiety can show up at different points for a single situation: You're an actor. Prior to auditioning for a play, you picture the audition going wrong: *Should I even show up? What if I mess up?* (This is imposter anxiety happening *before* the activity.) Then, the moment when the casting director's eyes lock on you, your body stiffens. You think: *Here it is. This is when he finds out I'm not supposed to be here.* (This is imposter anxiety showing up *during* the activity.) Then, on your car ride home, you shake your head in dismay: *I can't believe I even went there. He must be thinking that I'm a horrible actor.* (This is imposter anxiety coming up *after* the activity.) Self-doubt can be present every step of the way. But it manifests differently for each person walking through it. Your social identity, for instance, influences the way you navigate imposter anxiety (Bastian 2019).

When Imposter Anxiety Intersects with Your Social Identity

Your social identity has to do with your group memberships in society. This includes your gender group, racial group, age group, and so on. Entering spaces where you feel outnumbered, underrepresented, or like the only one of your kind can bring about imposter anxiety: like being the only person— or one of the few—from your age group, the only Black person, the only trans person, and so on.

Consider the gender makeup of a group to illustrate this. Picture a female engineer in an organization made up mostly of men. She doesn't feel like she belongs in this male-dominated space, and this leads her to question, *Will they understand me? What if they judge me because I'm a woman?* In chapter 7, you'll gain tools to delight in your difference even when you're outnumbered in a space.

> **CHECKING IN**   When did you feel out of place because there wasn't enough representation of people like you in the group?

How Your Personality Influences Imposter Anxiety

Your personality is another aspect of your social identity. Your personality or temperament is your natural way of being. It's your preferred mode of interacting with the world. Although imposter anxiety isn't limited to people of certain temperaments, your personality can influence how you maneuver it. Think about whether you lean towards being introverted or extroverted. If you gain energy by being around others, then you're likely extroverted. But if you gain energy by spending time in solitude, then you fall more on the introverted side. This doesn't mean that introverts never enjoy mixing and mingling or that extroverts never appreciate their quiet time.

Knowing where you fall on the introvert-extrovert continuum can give you insight into how you navigate imposter anxiety, especially when dealing with societal expectations associated with personality. Take the pressure to be extroverted in class, at work, or even in your own sanctuary, your home. Your participation grade is determined by how much you speak in class. New opportunities often get extended to the most socially involved team members at work. And when hosting guests at your home, you feel the weight of keeping your visitors entertained. Situations like these, where extroverted behaviors are expected or favored, make it difficult for introverts to feel okay with the way they're showing up in different social settings. Imposter anxiety complicates matters even more when it prompts you to take on a personality that isn't true to the real you. This goes for extroverts, too. If you're an extroverted person who feels more comfortable in group settings, self-doubt may strike when you're required to do things on your own. The bottom line is this: You can be introverted, extroverted, or anywhere on this spectrum and deal with imposter anxiety.

When facing fear and self-doubt, it's also possible to fall deeply into your preferred temperament. Take the experiences of Mike and Chaz to illustrate this. Mike is quiet and reserved. Chaz, on the other hand, is outspoken and sociable. Both are charged with the same task: to lead a group meeting. And both are working through imposter anxiety. Despite their shared experience with self-doubt, their reactions to it are different. Here's how each of their meetings play out:

Mike facilitates his meeting rather hastily to get it over with. He already dislikes speaking in front of large groups of people. His uneasiness drives him to round up the meeting quickly. He thinks that the sooner he ends it, the less time he'll need to stay in a situation where he feels like a fraud.

Contrary to Mike's reaction is Chaz's. Remember, Chaz is the one who feels comfortable expressing herself in group settings. But during her meeting, she talks much more than usual. She speaks in circles and spends too much time explaining her points. Chaz's talkative display is a manifestation of her struggle to appear more capable than she feels. She doesn't mean to be a chatterbox, but the overamplification of her natural disposition is an indicator of her insecure feelings while speaking.

Can you see how Mike's and Chaz's reactions are inflated displays of their usual temperaments? This example wasn't made to suggest that Mike's and Chaz's actions are standard behaviors of introverted or extroverted folks. Such reactions may or may not be a factor for you. But it's helpful to recognize how your personality can influence your manifestations of imposter anxiety.

CHECKING IN   How do you think your personality shapes the way you experience imposter anxiety?

So far, you've gotten a glimpse at some of the influences of imposter anxiety. How would you categorize these factors, though? Are they internal? Or are they external? Too often, the default has been to describe the phenomenon as an occurrence shaped by issues within you. Some others acknowledge it solely as a reaction to outside stimuli. Throughout the coming chapters, you'll see how imposter anxiety is a result of both internal and external factors.

Internal and External Forces

External stimuli are those triggers outside of yourself, like your environment, other people's behaviors, and societal norms. Social media is a major external force. It's a metaverse full of people's success stories and filtered images. You see others looking great and living their best lives. But imagine how these depictions could affect the way you feel about yourself. Like feeling unattractive or thinking you're not as accomplished as your peers.

As for *internal* influences of imposter anxiety, these include your mindset and beliefs. Your natural dispositions, like your survival instinct and personality, are also internal factors. But although your mindset and beliefs are internal stimuli of imposter anxiety, they are molded by external forces.

Here's a sample story to clarify this. As a child, the neighborhood kids laughed at you for the way you danced during a block party. Your interpretation of the encounter is *I'm an awful dancer.* You absorbed this message about yourself. Now, anytime there's a chance to dance at a gathering, you think twice. People laughing at you again is what you fear will happen. In this scenario, the laughing kids are the external stimuli. In fact, any other dance setting you're in after the incident is now an external trigger. As for the internal influence of your reactions, it's your *belief* about your dancing abilities. The past incident is the external force your current belief about your dancing is shaped by.

The inner and outer stimuli which imposter anxiety is activated by resemble the conversations around nature versus nurture: Is imposter anxiety *inherent* to us? Or does our *environment* play a role? Explore figure 1 for a better sense of the connections between all four factors.

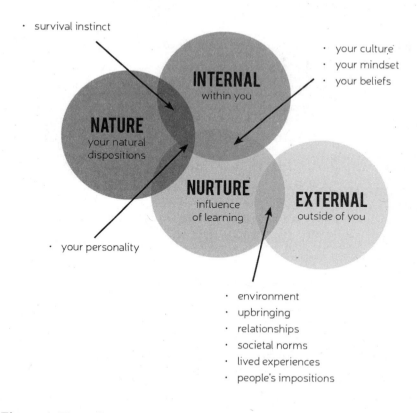

Figure 1: The Influences of Imposter Anxiety

Nature and Nurture Factors

Your nature is your inborn wiring and tendencies. Your survival instinct and your personality are both internal and nature influences. In chapter 3, you'll learn more about the relationship between your survival instinct and imposter anxiety. As for your personality, it's not only an internal and nature factor. Your personality is also shaped by what you learn in your life, making it nurture influenced as well. Here's how nature and nurture differ. Nature factors are inherent to you since your formation. But nurture influences happen after you were born. Nurture stimuli are external, like your environment, upbringing, relationships, social norms, and your lived experiences. But nurture factors, like your cultural practices, mindset, and the ideas you learned over time, become internal stimuli.

Throughout this book, you'll see how imposter anxiety is activated by both nature and nurture factors. But despite these influences, you are capable of moving past self-doubt when it strikes. I'll help you get there.

Impact on Your Health, Relationships, and Earnings

Let's look at how imposter anxiety can tamper with three important areas of your life: your health, your relationships, and your financial earnings.

Impact On Your Health

Health is wealth. With good health, you can be who you desire and go after what you want. But how can you thrive if imposter anxiety affects your well-being? Your body is indeed designed to handle small doses of stress. In fact, stress can prompt you to take positive actions. But dealing with high levels of stress from imposter anxiety can be problematic. This kind of stress takes a toll on your well-being. Because when big stress is activated too often and for too long, it is detrimental not only to your emotional health but also to your physical health.

Look at all the harm stress could lead to. It causes your heart to beat faster than normal. And when this happens for extended periods, it raises your blood pressure. Hypertension, then, becomes a possibility down the line. Stress also alters your digestive health, and you could lose your appetite. Or maybe the opposite happens, where you overindulge in comfort foods as a form of stress eating. Stress hormones drive unwanted weight gain and impair your body's immune system, making it tougher to recover from life's daily rigors. Acne, difficulty concentrating or sleeping, hair loss, head and stomach pains, persistent tiredness, and irritability—these are also the effects of stress. But when you take steps to surmount imposter anxiety, you can free yourself from the multitude of harm this reaction could wreak on your overall well-being.

> **CHECKING IN**   How has stress from imposter anxiety affected your health?

Impact on Your Relationships

Let's say you want to form closer friendships with certain people, but you feel inadequate around them. What do you do? You might pretend to be someone you're not. You might hold back in speaking openly with them. You might avoid asking them for help. Or you might share on a surface level without revealing the details of what you're going through. But if you limit yourself in these ways, won't it be difficult to form the heart-to-heart connections you desire?

Picture this scenario as well. You are overly reliant on a companion of yours. You look to this person to make up for what you believe are your shortcomings. This kind of relationship is a *codependent* one, rooted in self-doubt. But when you do the work to move past imposter anxiety, you can nurture healthy, *interdependent* relationships. These are connections where you know your value as well as the other person's. You believe in your capabilities just as you believe in the other person's. And you both work together without being needy of your companion's support.

Here's the main point. Healthy relationships are critical for overcoming fear and self-doubt. They help you achieve your life goals. They provide you with the encouragement you need to flourish. But imposter anxiety threatens these possibilities if left unaddressed. Chapter 11 is a deeper exploration of relationships as a means for overcoming imposter anxiety. There, you'll learn strategies to establish your very own network of support.

CHECKING IN   How do your insecurities about yourself affect your relationships?

Impact on Your Earnings

I'm sure you've imagined your ideal income multiple times before, or at least once. But what have you done with this dream? Did you abandon it because it wasn't "realistic"? Well, I've got news for you about "realistic" goals: they are driven by the thought of not being worthy or capable enough to achieve big aspirations. You may think you hold realistic perspectives about how much money you can earn. But "realistic" ideas about your earning potential keep you playing small and settling for less than what's possible for you. How can you earn what you desire if you undermine what you're worth or capable of?

It's like when you don't bother applying for jobs you've been eyeing. You don't negotiate your salary. You don't ask for a raise or promotion. You don't start the business you envision. You shortchange your skills. And despite your immense talent, you settle for low earnings.

Money can help you accomplish your life goals and acquire things that bring you joy. So how much longer will you let imposter anxiety discourage you from doing your part to earn your ideal income? You can reach your financial goals. But it won't happen until you overcome your self-doubts. This way, you're more empowered to embark upon more revenue-growing opportunities.

CHECKING IN   How might imposter anxiety be affecting your earnings?

Here are the main points to remember from this chapter:

- Imposter anxiety is normal anxiety. It's not an anxiety disorder.

- You can encounter imposter anxiety at different points throughout your life.

- Imposter anxiety can happen before, during, and after an activity or a situation.

- Your social identity influences how you experience imposter anxiety.

- Internal and external stimuli as well as nature and nurture factors spark imposter anxiety.

- Doing nothing about imposter anxiety can affect your overall well-being, your relationships, and your earnings.

This chapter gave you a broad glimpse at some of the facets of imposter anxiety. Now, let's go a bit further to understand the process of this phenomenon. Chapter 2 will give you first-class seating to learn the thoughts, emotions, and actions involved in this experience of fear and self-doubt. So, buckle your seatbelts. We're about to fly higher.

Thoughts, Feelings, and Behaviors of Imposter Anxiety

Dealing with imposter anxiety is like waiting on a diagnosis. Your attention gets derailed. You can't seem to focus on other things. Tummy flutters show up. And your breath is held hostage in your chest. Down a rabbit hole of panic is where you go. You ponder worst-case scenarios, feel trapped in uncertainty, and fixate on what could happen if you are "found out." Can you relate? For many people, this is what it's like to experience imposter anxiety. It's also a depiction of how your feelings impact what happens in your body. But let's explore this reaction more and look at the different ways imposter anxiety manifests. You can think of the experience as a process of moving through three domains: thoughts, feelings, and behaviors. With imposter anxiety, what thoughts circle your mind? What emotions and feelings come up for you? And what behaviors do you exhibit?

Thoughts

- *I'm unworthy.*
- *I don't belong.*
- *I'm not good enough.*

Feelings	Behaviors
• Afraid	• Push back
• Ashamed	• Escape
• Frustrated	• Shut down
• Powerless	• People-please

Self-Restrictive Thinking

What do you imagine when you picture *self-doubting thoughts*? You might think of those constricting ideas that pop into your head. You know, the ones you don't feel in control of when they show up. How about the *what if* questions you're confronted with during triggering moments?

What if they find out what I'm really like?

What if they think I'm unfit?

What if I'm doing this all wrong?

Perhaps these are the kinds of thoughts you have. But one thing about them is this: they come and go. And you'll see how they are a bit different from a *self-limiting mindset*. You form this mindset when you accept fear-based beliefs you've acquired over time about yourself. It's like having a set attitude about what you can do: you don't think you can improve in a particular area, so you don't even try to get better at it. When you investigate the root of your self-limiting mindset, you'll realize how your past experiences and memories shape these toxic beliefs.

Self-doubting thoughts and a self-limiting mindset are similar. They both exist within the thinking realm. But knowing how your thoughts contrast from your mindset can help you respond to them accordingly. Here's how to distinguish the two:

With a self-doubting thought, you don't necessarily accept these thoughts as what you believe, or your truth, as is the case with your mindset. You are more aware of your thoughts in the moment. But with your mindset, you may or may not be readily aware of the beliefs you hold and that end up guiding your actions. It's easier to fall into self-sabotaging behaviors with a self-limiting mindset, because negative ideas would have already been internalized. But with your thoughts, these ideas aren't necessarily absorbed into your psyche, so it's not as hard to dismiss them and to continue pursuing your personal goals. This chart will sharpen your understanding of the differences between self-doubting thoughts and a self-limiting mindset.

Self-Doubting Thoughts	Self-Limiting Mindset
You are aware of these thoughts in the moment.	You may or may not be readily aware of your beliefs.
These thoughts can come and go.	These beliefs are embedded in your mind.
You don't necessarily accept these thoughts as your truth.	You've accepted these beliefs as your truth.
You may not be easily swayed by these thoughts.	It's easier to fall into self-sabotaging behaviors since these beliefs are internalized.
These thoughts feel involuntary when they pop up in your mind.	You can choose to change your mindset once you're aware of it.
Responding to self-doubting thoughts effectively helps shift your mindset in a positive direction.	A self-limiting mindset affects the way you respond to self-doubting thoughts.

Despite their differences, self-doubting thoughts and a self-limiting mindset are intertwined. Your thoughts can feed your mindset just as your mindset influences your thoughts. So, you can consider the entire experience, of having self-doubting thoughts and a self-limiting mindset, as *self-restrictive thinking*. Have you experienced self-restrictive thinking in any of these ways?

- You are preoccupied about qualities you want to perfect, even when your abilities are already impressive. You dwell on setbacks, past mistakes, and critical feedback you received.

- You think you're unworthy of success. You believe factors like the appeal of your personality led to your wins, not your skills or intellect.

- You struggle with valuing your unique talents and your deeds. You imagine things like *They probably chose me because I smiled a lot during the interview* or *This organization only hired me because of who my father is, not because I'm qualified.*

- You don't see your victories as earned. Instead, you're convinced you were admitted into a prestigious program, or picked for an esteemed position, because you got lucky or the timing was right. But in the words of Seneca the Younger, "Luck is what happens when preparation meets opportunity." With self-restrictive thinking, you forget to acknowledge your act of preparing for success as one of the reasons you deserve it.

- You're skeptical about the positive feedback others give you. You don't think they mean what they say. So, you dismiss their praises and assume *They're just trying to be nice.* You take compliments from others with a grain of salt.

In the coming chapters, I'll equip you with tools to address self-restrictive thinking. You'll use these insights to establish an overcomer's mindset. For now, let's explore another aspect involved in the process of imposter anxiety: the *emotions* and *feelings* of this experience.

Emotions and Feelings of Imposter Anxiety

Ever thought about the difference between your feelings and emotions? You probably take them to mean the same thing, but differences exist between the two. With imposter anxiety, you can encounter any of these broad *emotions*: fear, shame, anger, and sadness. But there are loads of *feelings* linked to each of these emotions. Think of a feeling as the meaning you give to an emotion. For instance, feeling hesitant to speak up is rooted in the emotion of fear, and feeling inadequate is linked to the emotion of shame. Your feelings are more individualized than emotions. This is because your feelings are shaped by the way you think. Your thoughts and beliefs are what you use to make meaning of an emotion. So, your feelings are a mixture of your thought patterns and your emotions, making your feelings more specific and complex than emotions.

Here's the good news: you have the power to shape what you believe. Therefore, you can change your feelings. Your emotions are not as controllable because they don't involve any form of deeper reasoning (Grande 2018). They are simply your raw, immediate reactions to a trigger. And it's okay to experience them, because they are valid. A good thing about your emotions is they are fleeting. Nonetheless, it's important to manage what you have better control over and what is longer lasting if left unaddressed: your feelings.

As promised, you'll learn to reframe your thinking so you can dissolve the feelings you encounter from imposter anxiety. But first, get familiar with the types of feelings you could have when dealing with this reaction. The feelings listed here are grouped based on the emotions they are amplified by. Keep in mind, these are examples of imposter anxiety-related feelings, not a complete list.

Emotions	Feelings
Fear	*Afraid* to be my authentic self
	Hesitant to take bold strides toward my goals
	Insecure about my capabilities
	Nervous about speaking up
	Self-conscious about how others perceive me
	Skeptical about my ability to succeed
	Worried about my performance

Emotions	Feelings
Shame	*Ashamed* of my insufficient skills
	Embarrassed by my flawed speech
	Exposed as a fraud
	Foolish for thinking I could pursue a higher role
	Guilty for not saying the right things
	Inadequate because others have more experience than me
	Incapable of performing well
	Inferior because of the negative stereotypes about my identity group
	Insignificant because of what I haven't accomplished
	Unintelligent because of my limited knowledge
	Unworthy of reaching my big goals
Anger	*Disappointed* with myself for making a mistake
	Envious of other people's talents
	Frustrated with myself for not being good enough
Sadness	*Alone* in navigating imposter anxiety
	Discouraged about not yet grasping a concept
	Isolated because my identity group is outnumbered
	Miserable because of the burden of my self-limiting thoughts
	Out of place because I don't feel like I belong
	Overwhelmed by my doubts
	Powerless because of what I can't control

CHECKING IN Which of the feelings of imposter anxiety listed here have you encountered?

Self-Sabotaging Behaviors

You know what self-restrictive thinking is like. You're aware of the different feelings you can experience when dealing with imposter anxiety. Now here's what happens if those thoughts, beliefs, and feelings take the wheel: they will steer you directly toward *self-sabotaging behaviors*. This is the third domain of the process of imposter anxiety. Think of self-sabotage as those defensive actions you take (or don't take) in reaction to self-doubt. You make these gestures to guard yourself from being exposed. But self-sabotage prevents you from achieving your desires. You surrender to limiting beliefs. You stay in your comfort zone. You wait for perfection. Or you walk away from your dreams. The question to ask yourself is *How does denying myself in these ways serve me?* Self-sabotaging behaviors manifest in a variety of ways, but you can sort them as four types:

- Push back

- Escape

- Shut down

- People-please

The Pushback Reaction

"This can never happen again!" the department head declared. He reproached the team for overspending on the budget the year before. They were in the hole with a negative balance of thousands of dollars. After learning of this history, the director made a commitment not to allow the same mistake again. To create an efficient budget tracking system, she needed to get purchase receipts and other documents to cross-check the spendings so far. But gathering this information required Gina's help. She had the records the director needed.

Gina met the director's request with a hostile tone, opposing questions, short replies, and snarky retorts. The director wondered: *Why so much resistance? Shouldn't Gina feel relieved to have a better tool for tracking the budget?*

Wouldn't she want us to avoid repeating past overspending woes? Gina often grew defensive when asked for records she keeps up with. She worries her accounts of the budget are not up to par, so she doesn't want people to see the details of it. Gina's behaviors mirror pushback reactions to her feelings of inadequacy.

This is one of the four types of self-sabotaging behaviors.

In pushback mode, you behave aggressively in reaction to imposter anxiety. Your body may tense up, as if you're preparing for battle. In Gina's case, she was afraid of being viewed as a poor budget manager. How about you? Has imposter anxiety led you to push back? At some point, you may have enacted one or more of the many pushback reactions. Like stretching yourself thin trying to perfect a presentation. You don't want to appear incompetent in the eyes of those who will bear witness to your work. You could run through your presentation to the point of excellence. But in your mind, trying to perfect it is how you protect yourself. Spending excessive amounts of time practicing your delivery, over and over. But can it ever be perfect?

Pushback could also be your reaction when it comes to delegating responsibilities—you have a hard time doing it. You don't want others to think you're a bad leader if something goes wrong under your watch. So you take on all the duties on your own.

You also enter pushback mode when you think your significance or competence is being challenged, so you combat the thought by boasting about your past accomplishments. This is your attempt to make others see you as worthy.

Pushback could also be your reaction while conversing with your crew—you believe they don't take you seriously. With this concern in mind, you anticipate your turn to speak, just for a chance to look smarter than the people you're chatting with. You react to their views without listening to understand their points, rehearsing your replies in your head, then rattling off with the best comeback you can muster. Add a hostile tone of voice to your rebuttal and you've got yourself the perfect pushback reaction.

When grappling with imposter anxiety, you can push others, too. Bullying them, bossing them around, demanding special treatment, or pressuring others to meet your expectations. You find yourself micromanaging others. And without considering how your demands could be impacting their well-being, you require them to make no mistakes and produce nothing less than impeccable work. Your focus is to relieve your fear of being seen as less-than, even if it means disregarding the welfare of those around you. Intimidating people you view as threats and downplaying their talents are superiority-seeking gestures you make when you feel inferior.

A lot of these pushback reactions may seem over the top to you, especially the one about bullying. But as you can see, bullying as a pushback reaction is not far-fetched. That's how harmful imposter anxiety can be if you allow it to direct your actions.

CHECKING IN   Check your pulse on the following pushback behaviors:

- *I micromanage others because I fear failure.*

- *I avoid delegating tasks to others, because I fear people will think I'm incompetent if group goals aren't accomplished.*

- *I work extra hours to make my work flawless.*

- *I'm a bit hostile toward people when I feel like they are questioning my significance or competence.*

- *I undermine other people's qualities to make myself look better.*

- *I overextend myself to prove my worthiness.*

- *I act intimidating to gain power over others.*

- *I blow my own trumpet about past wins to appear better than others.*

The Escape Reaction

You might push back when triggered. Other times, you might attempt to leave those settings. This fleeing gesture is an *escape reaction*, a type of self-sabotaging behavior where you isolate yourself, or avoid, pull out, or hide from situations. It's like leaving a gathering early or arriving late just so you could miss certain imposter anxiety-provoking activities. Or dodging your chance to inquire about higher-level positions. You find excuses to refrain from going after something you want, saying things like *I don't have enough education for that job*. If you do start new endeavors, you give up prematurely. Or you might ghost people when you feel like you don't belong. *Ghosting* is when you disappear without an explanation. You stop communicating with someone or end your involvement with a group of people. In escape mode, you also shy away from showing confidence in what you're capable of. You do this to hide from accountability, because you're unsure if you can handle new or complex work. In your mind, displaying any degree of comfort about your skills means others will depend on you to take on bigger responsibilities. You escape to avoid being relied on.

Earlier, you read about the pushback reaction of handling tasks all on your own even when you have an opportunity to divide the work with others. Your reaction might be the opposite in escape mode, though, where in this case, you *are* willing to split duties, not because you are confident in your abilities but because you think you're not skilled enough to complete the work on your own. So you delegate tasks to share the onus. Your aim is to keep from taking all the blame if the efforts are a flop; you wouldn't be the only person at fault. If you had a choice, though, you'd prefer to not even be involved.

And how about the times when you desire help from others but you don't ask for it? This is another escape reaction. In this case, showing vulnerability by requesting support seems too risky to you. You think it exposes you as weak and in need of hand-holding. So you keep your struggles to yourself and suffer silently.

When you feel like escaping, your body also tries to escape. Notice how your body pulls inward to become small when you feel small. You might contort your body to move out of sight, like burying your head down at your desk in class, staring down at your notes to avoid eye contact with your instructor. You're afraid of being called on to share your thoughts in front of everyone. There are many other ways your body may attempt to take up less physical space. You might fold your arms, hide your tightly gripped hands under a desk, cross your ankles, slump over, pull your shoulders inward, and draw parts of your body closer toward your chest. These are all ways you make yourself less visible. It's as if you're entering a cocoon state, wrapping yourself up and closing your body off to the world. Your vocal expressions can shrink, too, like your tone changes or your voice gets shaky. In all, you may or may not be aware of what your body is doing when you pull back, because making yourself less noticeable can be both a conscious and subconscious reaction to feelings of inadequacy.

As you think about the way your body language reflects imposter anxiety, imagine the classic pose of superheroes as portrayed in the media. You've seen it. It's the stance exhibited by figures like Wonder Woman. She stands with her arms extended and her fingers formed into fists resting on her hips. Her chest up, chin lifted, and legs apart and planted firmly on the ground. When she speaks, her tone is strong and certain. Her gestures signify her dominance. She is sure she can save the day. In Amy Cuddy's popular 2012 TED talk, she refers to this superhero stance as a "power pose." You can easily recognize the meaning behind the power poses of fictional characters. But research findings go deeper in explaining the reality of this stance. What's been found is an expanded posture can reveal a person's feeling of power, while shrinking motions suggest a person's feeling of powerlessness.

It was 2003 when two researchers, Tiedens and Fragale, conducted experiments to investigate this dynamic. They studied the relationship between dominant and submissive nonverbal behaviors in humans, and here's what they discovered. Most of their subjects changed to more submissive posturing when they were exposed to a person displaying superiority.

The subjects did not mirror the stance of the person they were interacting with but instead exhibited the opposite posture. They took on a more submissive stance, constricting their bodies and making themselves small. The results were the same when the scenario was switched. Subjects who were exposed to a submissive person expanded how they expressed themselves and took on a more dominant posture. So, what do Tiedens and Fragale's studies tell you? Think of how you behave in different social settings. Could the gestures of the people you're around stir up your escape reactions? Do you shrink when surrounded by folks you believe hold more power than you?

CHECKING IN   Have you experienced any of these escape behaviors?

- *I make myself small when I feel inadequate.*

- *I stay away from spaces where I'm expected to participate.*

- *I leave gatherings early or join later to avoid certain activities.*

- *I dodge opportunities to pursue new and challenging undertakings.*

- *I disconnect from others when I feel like I don't belong.*

- *I avoid showing confidence to keep others from relying on me.*

- *I delegate tasks to reduce my responsibility over work I feel incapable of performing well.*

The Shutdown Reaction

When you can't push back or escape, you *shut down*. This standstill reaction happens when you're unsure of your next move. You become unresponsive, like a person who describes that they froze in their tracks. Your body stiffens. You hold your breath. Your body movements slow down or cease. The expression on your face might even seem stuck. And when your fears and self-doubts are intense and ongoing, you feel numb. Can you picture what emotional numbness is like? Think of it as motionless posturing, or having a flat affect, possibly showing no emotions. You can freeze when you're overwhelmed by imposter anxiety. Activities like taking a test or giving a talk are known to spark this reaction.

Disengaging is a type of shutdown behavior. Whether you want to participate in a conversation or not, you simply don't. You stay quiet to protect yourself from saying the wrong things. *Being indecisive* is another shutdown reaction. In this state, you struggle with choosing: *Should I pick a, b, c, or d?* Rather than trusting in yourself to make sound decisions, you're more concerned about what others will think about you. Then you get sidetracked. You end up focusing more on your worries than the task at hand: *Will they think my decision is dumb? What if they don't like the options I offer?* These doubts send you into a freeze-mode frenzy. Without committing to a side or a direction, you remain in limbo.

Procrastinating is a shutdown reaction with some escape energy behind it. It's often activated when you feel like you're all over the place and you have no idea where to start. You're unsure of what to do to achieve the right results, so you press the pause button on your actions. You're afraid you might mess up if you keep going. Here's one student's experience with procrastination. Reply drafts to her professors' emails were left pending. This became a pattern. "I don't want to come across as crass," she worried. "I'm not sure if my tone is polite enough." Rather than actively working on her replies, she spent a significant amount of time fretting over what to write, leading to delays in sending out her emails. You can see how freezing up disrupted her progress. But, for you, how have shutdown behaviors kept you from getting things done?

CHECKING IN   Which of these shutdown reactions can you relate to?

· *I become unresponsive.*

· *I become silent.*

· *I become indecisive.*

· *I procrastinate.*

The People-Pleasing Reaction

The fourth type of self-sabotaging behavior is *people-pleasing*. Because you're concerned about being liked, you alter your gestures to appease folks you believe are more important, powerful, or talented than you are. You might feel anxious. But despite this feeling, you put on your happy face to mimic an upbeat attitude. You change your tone of voice to sound welcoming, smiling more than you'd like and bending over backwards to accommodate others. These are all typical people-pleasing traits. But look at the different categories of this type of self-sabotaging behavior. You can act like a yes-man, praise others excessively, downplay yourself, and code-switch. Let's take a closer look at each of these roles.

THE YES-MAN

"I'm not a deep thinker like my friends." Jamari spoke about navigating imposter anxiety in his inner circle. His friends expressed strong opinions about political hot topics each time they got together. But Jamari felt like he didn't know enough about world issues to form his own perspectives on them. He feared his friends would reject him or view him as an enemy. So Jamari became a yes-man around them, nodding his head and pretending to agree with every opinion they asserted. He was sad about how out of place he felt around the people he yearned to be himself with. Think about what it would be like for you if you were in Jamari's shoes. Do you think you'd feel a heavy sensation in the pit of your gut? Would you long to unleash your real thoughts in those moments?

As a yes-man, you say yes too often. *Yes, I agree. Yes, I'll cover your shift. Yes, I'll pick up the refreshments from the store for you. Yes, I'll go ahead and pay for everything.* Being viewed positively is what you want to maintain. So, you don't challenge folks to reconsider their ideas, even when you see other promising solutions. You yield to people's whims and accept their views without question. At your job, for example, the work you agree to do is misaligned with your values, and the duties you're charged with are outside your scope of responsibility, falling either above or below your pay grade. But appealing to your boss or your team is your concern. So, you stay busy, work beyond your designated hours, and hope they'll see you as a valuable member of the group.

Agreeing to everything may seem like a way to feel emotionally secure, but it can lead to the opposite. People may take advantage of you if they see that you always say yes. Some want to keep you as their yes-man, but being one only makes others overload you.

Chase always agreed to everyone's requests, even his boss Richard's request to work on his paid time-off day. The reason for this? So Richard could meet a deadline he himself had procrastinated on! But Richard's lack of planning should not become an emergency for Chase. Despite always saying yes, Chase never received any promotion or salary adjustment from Richard.

While being a yes-man may temporarily benefit some people, it's not favorable in the long run. You may find yourself enacting this people-pleasing gesture to survive your environment. This is valid. But know this: being a yes-man can be a way of disrespecting yourself and may not promote self-confidence or self-care. So, the question to ask yourself is this: what healthy gain do you acquire by saying yes to people's boundary-crossing requests?

CHECKING IN   What do you say yes to when you know it ought to be a "no, thanks"? How is this reaction harmful to you?

THE FLATTERER

You might be someone who usually speaks your mind, even when you want to make bold statements, but once you get around a person you feel insecure around, you put on your flatterer hat. You don't want to be cast out for sharing your genuine thoughts. So you withhold your truth and suppress the constructive feedback you could have offered. You pour out flattering words about the other person instead, praising their skills and deeds. When you think you don't add much value to your group, you feel obliged to say something, so you fill the void by lavishing compliments onto others. This is your attempt to remain in their good graces or to contribute in whatever way you can.

CHECKING IN   Have you ever praised someone excessively to offset your feelings of inadequacy?

THE DOWNPLAYER

Discrediting your strengths and good deeds is to downplay yourself. You believe what you have to offer is insignificant, so you either avoid talking about your qualities or you downplay them. When people undermine you, you don't try to correct them. You also have a hard time viewing yourself as worthy but succeed at seeing others as such. In the downplayer role, you adopt flatterer tendencies, inflating the perspectives of others while deflating your own ideas. Dismissing yourself in these ways suggests this. You trust others more than you trust yourself. But how does discounting yourself honor you?

CHECKING IN   In your life, when do you downplay yourself? Journal about why this was your reaction.

THE CODE SWITCHER

Jeff, an African American man, feels pressure to conform to White norms in order to be accepted by his colleagues and avoid negative stereotypes associated with his natural way of speaking. At a happy hour with his White colleagues, Jeff modifies his speech to match their way of talking, despite feeling uneasy about doing so.

Jeff's gesture of changing the way he speaks is known as code switching. This is when you swap between different ways of communicating. Code switching isn't always activated by imposter anxiety. It could also be your way of embracing multiple aspects of your authentic self when you're around the different groups you belong to. But code switching as a people-pleasing reaction is produced by the opposite. The desire to code-switch can kick in when you feel like you don't belong but you want to fit in. Switching code under these circumstances is like walking on eggshells. Jeff is trying to enjoy the company of his colleagues. At the same time, he's striving to make sure his way of speaking sends a message to the others that he belongs. Jeff feels stressed and drained from juggling both efforts at once.

CHECKING IN   Do you find yourself code switching in certain spaces? Is it energizing or exhausting?

At the checking-in points in this chapter, you probably realized that you've encountered many of the imposter anxiety–related thoughts, feelings, and behaviors described. You may also notice that you haven't faced some others. This is because your circumstances influence what imposter anxiety looks like for you. You'll learn how different situations stir up self-doubt throughout this book. But for the next chapter, I'll unveil the role your survival instinct plays in your experience with imposter anxiety.

CHAPTER 3

Responding to the Inner Disrupter

Imagine a person whose paranoia causes them to avoid new ventures, steer clear of growth opportunities, and criticize themselves constantly. This person happens to be your advisor, and you want them to guide you in reaching your goals. But when you meet with your advisor, their feedback to you is based in fear. They discourage you from taking risks and moving away from the familiar. They harp on all the things that could go wrong, without acknowledging what could go right. How helpful can they be? It would be next to impossible to achieve your dreams with an advisor like this. Now, think of your self-doubting thoughts as the voice of that advisor. You recognize its chatter. It's persistently harsh, worried, judgmental, and, most importantly, inaccurate. It says, *You are undeserving, your difference is a weakness, you are incompetent, you are a failure, your efforts don't matter, you are the problem*—the list goes on. That voice is *the inner disrupter*. It's the force behind your experiences with imposter anxiety. But to understand why the inner disrupter exists in the first place, let's explore the science behind it.

All Risk Seems Like Bad Risk

As a human, you were born with a self-preservation instinct. Its goal is to help you survive. And it aims to shield you from harm, inciting fears within you to keep you away from potential risks or the unknown (Mobbs et al. 2015). This function of your survival instinct sounds favorable, right? Well, it is. Because these reflexes help alert you of physical dangers. There's a snag, though. Your safety instinct doesn't always understand the assignment. It detects physical hazards as risks, as it should. But the problem is it interprets beneficial challenges as risks, too. This means healthy risks, or good growth opportunities, get clumped together with actual dangers. And this is why your safety instinct dissuades you from approaching positive activities as it does with life's real hazards. Can you see how your natural defenses can be misleading? Your instinctive reactions could drive you away from promising paths. When you give in to them, you rob yourself of chances to follow your ambitions.

The Threat of Emotional Risk

Your safety instinct activates the inner disrupter to deter you from moving forward with new or challenging activities. Indeed, there's a "risk" your instincts detect when you're stretching yourself into your personal best. It's an *emotional* risk. Like the risk of feeling embarrassed if you're exposed as a fraud. Remember the self-sabotaging behaviors described in chapter 2, like push back, escape, shut down, and people-please? These defensive reactions are your instinct's attempts to guard you from being "found out." But what can you do to manage these reactions when you're partaking in good growth opportunities? The inner disrupter is an offshoot of your survival instinct; you can't necessarily stop it from showing up. However, you can certainly take steps to overcome it.

CHECKING IN   Describe the emotional risks you're worried by when you're presented with challenging growth activities. Do you fear embarrassment? Failure? Exposure? Vulnerability?

Overcoming the Inner Disrupter

My use of the word "overcome" may or may not be what you have in mind. To be clear, overcoming the inner disrupter isn't about eliminating it from your thoughts, causing it to never show up in your life again. Your safety instinct is part of your natural human functioning, so you will continue to encounter the inner disrupter at different points throughout your life. And it's possible to move past the inner disrupter in one setting, then experience it again when you enter a different situation. Overcoming the inner disrupter is about moving beyond that voice by *responding effectively* when it shows up. This requires you to adopt the mindset and approach of an overcomer. I'll illustrate this by sharing the story of Kyra. Through her story, you'll see how she prevailed over the inner disrupter.

Story: Kyra the Pilot

Meet Kyra. She's a forty-year-old mother of three small children, who longed to become a pilot since she was a kid. Coming from a lineage of aviators, Kyra drew inspiration from her older brothers, who were all pilots. She was twenty years old when she first set out to become an aviator. But after graduating from college, she decided to "play safe and small," and choose a more "stable," traditional corporate career track. This kept her "safe" on the ground, and out of the air. But in the air was truly where she longed to be.

Fast-forward twenty years later: Kyra's dream of becoming a pilot still lived. So she decided to try again. She enrolled in flight school. This took her one step closer to fulfilling her longtime desire. But she was now faced with a new set of circumstances. She described a demanding home life: cooking, cleaning, feeding, caregiving, piles of laundry, errands, the list goes on. She felt engulfed by these duties, and they evoked self-doubting thoughts in Kyra again. She not only was on edge about her role at home but also dealt with doubts around her ability to fly a plane without a copilot. She had to showcase this skill to earn her pilot license.

Earlier, you learned that the inner disrupter appears in situations where risks are involved. Being seen as a bad mother for her career choice is what the inner disrupter pointed out as the emotional risk for Kyra. But she grappled with the physical risks of flying, too. Her angst around the emotional and physical threats clashed with her longing to become a pilot. She couldn't decide: *Should I fly or should I not?* Kyra sought to cancel the inner disrupter's influence over her decision. So, I guided her along the following steps to respond to the inner disrupter the right way.

1. Detect the inner disrupter.

2. Accept its inevitability.

3. Treat it like a separate entity.

4. Handle it with kindness.

5. Identify the facts.

6. Recognize the opportunities.

7. Do the opposite of what it suggests.

1. DETECT THE INNER DISRUPTER

After Kyra laid out her main concerns, I helped her identify the disrupter's presence in her situation. Here are its messages to her:

You have too much going on at home.

You don't deserve to be a pilot.

Why are you pursuing such a risky career?

Your kids need you alive.

You're not a good mother if you enter this dangerous field.

Kyra spotted the inner disrupter's voice by paying attention to her conflicting views. Her discord came from juggling two opposing ideas: she wanted to become a pilot, but the inner disrupter told her being a pilot would make her a bad mother. Kyra recognized the ideas about staying away from her dream career as the voice of the inner disrupter.

You can pinpoint the disrupter in your own life by noticing moments where you feel conflicted and insecure.

2. ACCEPT THE INNER DISRUPTER'S INEVITABILITY

After Kyra detected the inner disrupter, she needed to recognize its inevitability. This means the inner disrupter is activated outside of your control, because it's a normal part of your existence. This was important for Kyra to understand for a few reasons. First, it could keep her from absorbing inaccurate views about who she is. She realized that her run-ins with the disrupter didn't mean she was a coward. Instead, the disrupter showed up naturally because she was immersed in a challenging situation. Second, by accepting the inner disrupter as an expected voice, Kyra could equip herself to respond to it correctly rather than believing it. Your ability to predict the disrupter enables you to stop it from influencing your decisions.

CHECKING IN   You can address the inner disrupter by responding to it differently. How does knowing this make you feel?

3. TREAT THE INNER DISRUPTER LIKE A SEPARATE ENTITY

Have you noticed how I refer to this voice as *the* inner disrupter, not *your* inner disrupter? I do so because the disrupter isn't solely encountered by you—or anyone. It's common to all humanity, not unique to you, so don't adopt it as who you really are. Your authentic self, however, is one of a kind, and therefore separate from the disrupter.

For Kyra, the disrupter would have had her believing she was an unfit pilot and parent. She needed to distinguish who she truly is from what the disrupter said she is. The real Kyra is a high-potential aviator who loves to fly and a responsible mother who is destined to accomplish her long-time career goal.

When the disrupter attempts to limit you, remind yourself of the real you; you are limitless and full of possibility. Your passions, talents, curiosities, and aspirations make up the real you. The real you wants to embrace your ambitions. The real you longs to do more and achieve more. The real you desires to unlock your infinite capacity to thrive. But the real you will remain trapped if you surrender to the directives of the inner disrupter. The disrupter isn't part of the real you. So regard its ideas as untruths and misrepresentations.

4. HANDLE THE INNER DISRUPTER WITH KINDNESS

Other teachings will advise you to overcome your "inner critic" by rough-handling it. You've probably heard of some of the ideas, like *tackle* self-doubt, *kill* imposter syndrome, or *fight* your fear. But rather than warring with the inner disrupter, it's better to respond to it with kindness. There's no need to be aggressive toward a mechanism that is only trying to keep you safe. So, show your understanding and appreciation for it by being kind to it. This doesn't mean you surrender to its fear-based narratives. Rather, treat its alerts only as reminders to handle "risky" goals with care while pursuing them.

Kyra had some jitters around being a newly minted pilot. But during our chat, she revealed the irony of who is usually involved in flight accidents. New pilots are the ones people assume would get into accidents right away. But Kyra described how accidents tend to happen among more seasoned pilots who had gotten used to flying, supposed that all will be well because they've flown over and over, and skipped going through safety checklists before taking flight. Checklists help pilots catch errors before they become big problems during critical moments of a flight. Kyra used the disrupter's presence as a cue to follow flight checklists rather than allowing it to overwhelm her. Instead of fighting against the disrupter, which can be self-sabotaging, Kyra harnessed its voice to help her stay focused on the important procedures she needed to complete. By viewing the disrupter as a prompt to follow her checklists, Kyra was able to maintain her composure and stay on track, ultimately ensuring that her flights are safe and successful.

Another way to handle the disrupter properly is to flip the way you interpret its claims. When it tells you, *You're too old, You're too young, You're not cool enough, You're not smart enough, You're not qualified, It's too competitive out there,* or *You're not ready to lead others,* interpret these messages as signs of success. They are clues, indicating to you that you are about to enter promising paths. Be empathic and grateful for the disrupter's communication as it attempts to guard you against harm. Tell it, *I understand your concern. Thank you for trying to protect me. But I'm choosing to move forward.* By gracefully approaching the disrupter, you can transform a potentially distressing situation into an empowering one.

5. IDENTIFY THE FACTS

After several trips in the air, Kyra's flight instructor assured her, "You're doing great. I think you're ready to go solo." Despite her instructor's confidence, Kyra felt nervous about her ability to fly without a partner. To help her feel less nervous about flying alone, we looked at the facts around it.

Kyra's main worry was engine failure, but her training had taught her how to handle the situation. Even if the engine stopped working, she could still fly the plane like a glider and safely land it. She achieved this many times during her training, when her instructor would simulate engine failure by pulling the engine throttle back to idle, leaving Kyra to execute the safe landing procedures she had learned.

So, the lesson here is this. The risks involved in the activities you want to pursue may not be as uncontrollable or enormous as you think. The inner disrupter is pretty good at making you believe otherwise. But when the inner disrupter dishes its drama, lay out the facts of the matter and use that intel to press forward in what you want to do. Ask yourself:

What are the facts?

Is this as risky as the inner disrupter makes it seem?

What's within my control?

The clarity you gain from identifying the facts of your situation can increase your willpower to take flight (pun intended) in reaching for the stars.

6. RECOGNIZE THE OPPORTUNITIES

Kyra had a busy home life, and she struggled to find time to focus on her exam: "How will I be able to pass? I don't have uninterrupted time to prepare for it." As Kyra expressed this worry, she didn't realize the significance of what she disclosed next: "My instructor said I could stay at her house while I complete the program. She's also the president of the flight school. It's out of town and hours away. I would be gone for a week—that's how long the program lasts." Presented right before Kyra's eyes was the solution to her concerns.

But in the way was the inner disrupter, blocking Kyra from taking stock of the opportunities handed to her and ready for her to grab hold of: "But I don't want to leave my kids for a whole week. I'm worried about them getting injured or not being taken care of properly while I'm away."

Kyra's fears are valid. But to help her avoid another dream delay, I reminded her of the many ways her instructor's proposal could put her on a fast track to accomplish her career goal. Staying at her instructor's home would give Kyra a space to focus without distractions. And attending the weeklong flight school would be a chance to spend ample time preparing for her license. Kyra would get hands-on support and consistent feedback from her instructor, providing her with the accountability she craved. She would also have access to a plane to practice with daily. Training each day would reduce the likelihood of forgetting what she learned and improve her comfort with flying. This would help build Kyra's confidence in flying solo. Enrolling in the accelerated program would also allow her to finish the training and licensing process faster. And when she was done with the program, she could use her free time to fulfill other important activities she wanted to tend to, like spending quality time with her family.

Kyra's kids were overjoyed by the fact that their "mommy is a pilot!" This was Kyra's chance to embrace her children's excitement and turn it into an opportunity. Instead of feeling like a bad parent for her chosen profession, Kyra involved her children in her career by taking them to air shows and monthly plane washes (complete with donuts!). By including her kids in her pilot world, she was able to show herself that she was a good mother who could inspire her children by bringing her career vision to life.

Kyra also changed her perspective around being gone for a week. She started seeing her out-of-town trip as an ideal opportunity rather than lost time from her kids. This was evident when I asked, "What is it worth to you, to spend seven days away in exchange for a lifetime in a fulfilling profession?" Kyra's response was, "It's priceless."

Accepting her instructor's offer and allowing her children to be her cheerleaders turned out to be worthwhile for Kyra. Her positive response to the inner disrupter propelled her to complete flight school without carrying the guilt of leaving her family to do so. Like Kyra, you can turn what the disrupter says is a disadvantage into your advantage. Do so by viewing your challenging situations through a new lens, recognizing the endless opportunities these experiences offer.

7. DO THE OPPOSITE OF WHAT THE INNER DISRUPTER SUGGESTS

Picture what could have happened if Kyra hadn't responded to the disrupter effectively. Would she wake up every morning filled with remorse for not pursuing her ideal career? Would feelings of emptiness keep her from showing up as the mom and spouse her family needed? Kyra took action to avoid these negative outcomes. She recognized that she was equipped to fly. She allowed her family to be her motivators. She completed flight school. She earned her pilot license. And as a result, Kyra achieved her ultimate desire: to demonstrate to her children that they too can fulfill their own big dreams.

Living out your greatest aspirations is attainable for you as well. Even when the inner disrupter rears its head, you can adopt the approach of an overcomer. This requires a deliberate effort to live your life by design, not by default. Living by default gives the disrupter permission to rule. But to live by design, you're intentional about going after your goals despite the disrupter's chatter. When it tells you to avoid, shrink, or flee, do the *opposite* of what it declares. This means you expand yourself instead of playing small. You voice your opinions, take initiative, or be truer to yourself.

Taking healthy risks is the path to fulfilling your ambitions. Be willing to climb the mountain of possibility, look over the valley of risk—with courage in one hand and your aspirations in the other—and leap toward the mountain of victory. When you do what it takes to reach your goals, you eliminate future regret. You wouldn't have to wonder: *What would my life have been had I dismissed the inner disrupter?* So, allow the seven steps to guide you in leaning into who you desire to be.

A Guide for Responding to the Inner Disrupter

Whenever you need to work through your experiences with the inner disrupter, turn to this page. Apply this process to any situation you face to respond to the disrupter effectively.

1. Detect the inner disrupter. In this situation, how can you tell the disrupter has paid you a visit? What self-doubts is it raising?

2. Accept the inner disrupter's inevitability. Acknowledge that the disrupter is present because you are taking on a challenging or unfamiliar endeavor.

3. Treat the inner disrupter like a separate entity. Distinguish the disrupter's messages from the qualities you believe to be true about yourself. Try writing this down. Make a list of what the disrupter is telling you. Next to it, write why those ideas are incorrect. You can also form another list of positive facts to dispel the disrupter's claims.

4. Handle the inner disrupter with kindness. Show some grace to the disrupter by saying something like *I appreciate your effort to shield me, but I'm making the choice to proceed.*

5. Identify the facts. Assess whether the pros of moving forward outweigh the risks involved. Ask yourself, *Is this really as threatening as the disrupter says? What's within my control? What will happen if I don't pursue what I want?*

6. Recognize the opportunities. Point out the opportunities this situation presents. Write those benefits down and meditate on them.

7. Do the opposite of what the inner disrupter suggests. Think of counter actions to reverse the disrupter's insinuations. In this situation, what would it look like for you to do the opposite of what the disrupter is urging you to do?

Situations Activating the Inner Disrupter

In this chapter, you learned how to identify and respond to the inner disrupter. This voice is set in motion by several factors. Triggers like these activate it:

- oppressive environments
- negative views of yourself
- feeling inexperienced
- comparing your unique attributes
- an unchecked ego
- competitiveness
- fear of failure
- lack of support

Wondering how each of these factors fuels fear and self-doubt? We'll take deeper dives to explore each of them in the chapters to come. Starting with the next chapter, I'll reveal how oppressive environments play a huge role in your experience with imposter anxiety.

CHAPTER 4

Recognize the Impact of Oppressive Environments

Despite widespread assumptions, a main culprit of your experience with imposter anxiety is not from inherent issues within you. It is, instead, found in sources *around* you (Tulshyan and Burey 2021). A memorable scene from the Oscar-winning film *Good Will Hunting* portrays this. Will, a young man who survived childhood physical abuse, had bottled up pain his foster father inflicted on him. Because of that period in his life, he put up defenses to shield himself from further emotional harm. But these barriers were sabotaging his life pursuits. Will had a breakthrough, however, during his final meetup with Sean, a psychologist, when Sean told Will, over and over, that the emotional injuries he suffered from his childhood were not his fault. Will bursts into a heavy bawl, releasing the pain he had internalized and carried for so long. Calling out Will's wounds as the wrongdoing of an external source helped Will progress past his emotional anguish. And by the end of the movie, we learn that Will goes after an important romantic relationship he once dodged because of the impact of the harm imposed on him by his foster father.

So, what is the connection between this scene from *Good Will Hunting* to your experience with imposter anxiety? Your tendency may be to look inward to blame yourself for your self-doubts. Others may even say you are the problem. But know this. Your feelings are the result of the impositions of your surroundings. My message to you, then, mirrors Sean's affirmations to Will. External forces, like oppressive environments, instill fear and self-doubt in you (Gildersleeve, Croom, and Vasquez 2011). So, remember, imposter anxiety is *not your fault*.

CHECKING IN   How does it feel to know your experiences with imposter anxiety are not your fault?

When You Are Imposterized

When your surroundings ignite your imposter anxiety, you are being *imposterized* (Robinson 2018). Unjust treatment by external sources gives rise to self-doubt. You get treated like an outsider. And you face unpleasant consequences for showing up as your authentic self. If you're being excluded, ignored, intimidated, silenced, unfairly blamed, or harshly criticized, it's not you who is the problem—it's the toxic setting you're in.

You can be imposterized in the different relationships and interactions you're involved in, by an individual or a group. These are the folks you're connected to through work, school, leisure, or any other setting. On a larger scale, you'll find other imposterizing sources in social structures, like the systems, practices, policies, standards, and cultures of your surroundings.

Here's the irony of being imposterized. You may very well be a confident person. You believe in what you can do, and you're eager to show up as your best self. But when others imposterize you, the positive views you hold about yourself get shaken. Imagine what it's like to know people in your circle are getting together, but no one invites you. And how you would feel if your peers were asked to help solve a problem, but you never receive a request to be a part of that process? Run-ins like this can tamper with how you feel about yourself, because you start to question if you even matter. This is what being imposterized is like with exclusion being one form of it. Being made to feel like you lack knowledge is another. It's like being in a class where your professor is talking about the experiences of a particular population. You are part of the demographic group he's describing. So, he assumes you know what the experience he's referring to is like. Your professor fails to acknowledge that people of a certain population aren't all the same. Your professor gazes at you, expecting you to respond. But you give a blank stare and wonder, *Why is he singling me out right now?* You don't relate to the ideas he seems to be imposing on you. And you're unsure of what to do. You're left feeling exposed and embarrassed in front of your classmates.

CHECKING IN   Write about a time when you felt confident going into an experience, but you left feeling insecure about yourself. How did your environment activate self-doubt in you?

Social Roots of Feeling Inferior

When you're imposterized, an outside source is attempting to gain control or exert power over you. They hold what makes you different against you, so you can doubt yourself. Because the idea is, if you feel inferior, then they can feel superior. Your social identities are the main areas imposterizers use to undermine you. To be clear on the meaning of social identity— it's your group membership in society. Your age, education level, ethnicity, gender, citizenship status, professional level, disability status, race, religion, sexual orientation, and socioeconomic status make up your social identity. You can also identify by your preferences, personality, and circumstances.

For each identity category, you fall in one of two groups. Your identity group is either dominating or subordinated in society. Keep in mind, I didn't say "dominant" or "subordinate." Saying so would imply that these groups are inherently superior or inferior. I say *dominating* and *subordinated* to acknowledge the imposed nature of these biased categories. These classifications are not so much about which group is bigger or smaller in size. And it's not about separating "better" identity groups from the "less-than" ones.

These groups are identified as dominating and subordinated to distinguish them based on their privilege in society. In this case, the idea of privilege is not about merit. It's about the access, power, and assets you have because of your identity group. And oftentimes, these privileges are unearned.

It's important to be aware of your identity groups, because your experiences with imposter anxiety are likely influenced by your dominating and subordinated identities. This chart, adapted from a Social Justice Training Institute training I attended some years back, gives you examples of the social structure in the United States. It's a limited list; other identity categories exist. But see where you fall for each category provided in the chart.

Social Structure in the United States

Identity Category	Dominating Group	Subordinated Group
Ability status	able-bodied	persons with physical or mental disabilities/ chronic illnesses
Age	thirties to fifties	younger than thirty; older than fifty
Behavioral style	extroversion	introversion
Educational level	college degree or higher; private school	high school or less; public school
Ethnicity	"American"; Western European	Navajo; Mexican; Ethiopian; Iranian
Gender identity	cisgender	transgender; gender nonconforming
Immigration status	United States citizen	undocumented in the United States
Professional level	senior level	entry level; student
Race	White	people of color; multiracial; biracial
Religion/spirituality	Christian	Muslim; Hindu

Identity Category	Dominating Group	Subordinated Group
Sex assigned at birth	male	female; intersex
Sexual orientation	heterosexual	lesbian; gay; bisexual
Socioeconomic status	middle to upper class	working class

Adapted from Social Justice Training Institute

This structure is our reality. And numerous studies continue to validate the existence of this unjust setup in society. Such a makeup comes from the history of racism, sexism, ableism, ageism, classism, ethnocentrism, and homophobia in the US—where straight wealthy White men design the systems, benchmarks, and values of our society. Here's the issue with these establishments: they were molded by stereotypes and biased beliefs dominating groups benefit from, while these setups imposterize subordinated identity groups. So, when your characteristics or ways of being don't match the standards set by dominating groups, you risk being seen as violating, or not being in alignment with, the norm. This is how the door of imposterizing is opened.

Coming up in this society, we've been conditioned to internalize inaccurate ideas about different identity groups. These opinions shape our culture. They inform rules and actions. They influence how we treat each other. And they determine who gets more freedoms to pursue life unreservedly. But if there's no real effort to get rid of imposterizing setups, then these ways of being end up perpetuated. The toxic messages of these structures seep into our psyche and form self-limiting views.

Now, take a moment to think of the role social disparities play in your experience with imposter anxiety. You can predict which identity group is likely to gain favor and which is likely to get overlooked. It's already challenging to navigate one subordinated identity—now, picture what living with more than one is like. Wouldn't dealing with imposter anxiety be even more complicated? Tommy's experience is a depiction of this. His story illustrates the imposterized experience of a person with multiple subordinated identities.

Story: Tommy

Tommy made his way to the trash bin, flung his plate in it, and left the event. After feeling the stares and hearing the whispers, Tommy couldn't stay any longer. He was at a welcome event for first-year students at his college, and he was looking forward to making new connections. At the event were seventeen- and eighteen-year-old traditional-aged students who appeared to be physically able-bodied. They conversed with one another, walking from person to person, mixing and mingling. Although Tommy has the same first-year status as the other students, he is visibly different from them. He's a fifty-five-year-old undergraduate, and he uses a wheelchair. His double subordinated status as a nontraditional-aged student and a person with a disability made him feel out of place. In observing the other students' demeanors, Tommy could see how perplexed they were by his presence. Barely anyone approached him. So, he decided to leave. Tommy *should* belong because of his first-year status, but because of his other subordinated qualities, he is left out.

CHECKING IN   How has your social identity been a factor in the way people treat you?

The Deep Pain of Being Excluded

"You shouldn't let what others say or do to you get to you" is what is often preached. This point can be helpful in some ways. But the truth of the matter is, being left out hurts. The cuts from mistreatment can run deep, like a physical wound. This is because the part of your brain that feels physical pain is the same part that processes emotional pain. So, the emotional harm of being imposterized is like being punched in the gut.

Kipling D. Williams, a psychology researcher, shared a real-life encounter he had that revealed this truth to him. He was at a park one day with his dog, minding his business. An object knocked him on the back. Kipling turned to see what it was when he noticed it was two guys playing frisbee. He threw the frisbee back to them. But just as he was about to return to sit on his blanket, one of the men tossed the frisbee back at him. He felt good for the moment—to be included in the game made him happy. So, he left his post to join the two men. All three of them started playing together, throwing the frisbee to one another. They played for a few minutes. But after that time passed, the two guys suddenly stopped tossing the frisbee to Kipling. He stood there watching both men enjoying themselves. They were no longer making eye contact with him or including him in the game. At first, Kipling thought they were just messing with him. But he stood there, watching them throw the frisbee back and forth to each other. Kipling finally realized the guys weren't going to toss the frisbee to him again. He felt immensely ashamed and slowly found his way back to his dog.

In hindsight, Kipling was surprised by how incredibly demoralized he felt for an activity that seemed so trivial. This irony fascinated him as a researcher. And it inspired him to study ostracism in his lab. Today, Kipling is known for his notable research on the topic. His studies confirmed what he had experienced that day at the park—that is, how social exclusion can drive feelings of unbelonging and emotional anguish (Williams and Nida 2011). If you're like Kipling, and you wonder why you feel emotional discomfort in imposterizing situations that seem so miniscule, here's what you should know: humans long to feel connected. We want to be valued. But these fundamental needs feel threatened when we are ostracized.

Being ostracized is like death. Death is a separation from the living. And when you're excluded or ignored, you're being separated from others. It prompts you to feel like your existence is meaningless. So, no matter how small you think a snub is, your feelings are legitimate. It doesn't matter if you're around people you know or complete strangers. It doesn't matter if your interactions are virtual or in person. It doesn't matter if you like or dislike the folks you're engage with. No matter the case, being ostracized hurts.

CHECKING IN   Write about a time you had an emotional reaction to an imposterizing situation that seemed trivial.

In life, you'll run into situations where you'll do what you think you need to do to keep your head above water in imposterizing environments. This can drive you to react with defensive behaviors like being passive-aggressive, leaving those spaces, being silent, conforming to norms, or trying to fit in.

Interestingly, there's a paradox in this. People who exclude or ostracize you oppress themselves, too. If they're looking to be big by making you small, they are feeding into a false sense of self. And they waste their time trying to imposterize you. Doing so could also leave them with little energy left to properly care for their emotional well-being, whether they're aware of it or not. And they block their chances of building a meaningful relationship with you. This is unfortunate, because relationships could enrich their lives. These connections could also help them gain new insights, and those ideas could inspire their creativity and innovation. You can picture this in Soya's story, and as you read through it, imagine the opportunities she *and* her team miss out on, all because her colleagues chose to imposterize her.

Story: Soya

Soya started off feeling good about the contributions she wanted to make in her new job. Her boss even told her, "We're lucky to have you on board." And her team shared their excitement, too: "We're so happy you're here." To welcome Soya, her organization threw a gathering, celebrating her with cake, signs, and balloons. Their warm gestures made Soya feel valued. And their support increased her willingness to speak up during meetings. She communicated her thoughts openly and felt comfortable giving constructive feedback. Soya had established herself as a competent leader. In her early days there, she showed her potential to transform the organization.

A few months passed when Soya began noticing changes in the support she received. She shared her perspectives with her team, and the room would become dead silent. This was followed by an interrogation of her suggestions by her colleagues. The opposite happened when her White colleagues expressed their sentiments, though. They were commended for their views. But when Soya spoke, her boss interrupted her. He gave ample airtime to others, and he barely made eye contact with Soya the way he used to.

Soya grew more anxious around her team. She turned inward to explore what she was doing wrong: *Am I too opinionated? Do they dislike my approach?* Despite her challenges at work, Soya persisted. She worked hard to perform well. And after being with her company for a couple of years, she anticipated a promotion. To her disappointment, she watched colleagues with less qualifications and experience climb to higher roles. She communicated her career advancement concerns to her boss. But he insisted that Soya be patient. He concocted reasons, like "We're waiting for a budget approval" and "There's a lot of politics involved in this, so we need to navigate this carefully." Soya felt seen when she first began her role. But months into it, she started feeling invisible. She had hoped to contribute her knowledge to move the organization forward. Instead, it's like Soya went from office *pet* to the office *threat*.

The Pet-to-Threat Phenomenon

Dr. Kecia M. Thomas, an expert in the psychology of workplace diversity, and her colleagues (2013), originated the phrase "pet to threat" to describe an experience like Soya's. This is when Black women in leadership are "liked" as long as they "stay in their place," like the treatment of a pet. With double subordinated identities, Black and woman, you can imagine the challenges a professional holding these identities has to navigate at work. Society sees straight White men as the avatar for leadership. They are thought to be the ones who should make decisions and hold the greatest power. So, when people witness Black women exhibiting qualities society ascribes to White men, they start viewing Black women leaders as threats. Threats to the mainstream culture and threats to norms. Imposterizing Black women at work is a tactic to put them "in their place." A place where they are void of decision-making power and influence. Like Soya, Black women professionals are the identity group that is likely to get undermined. Or disregarded. Or told to wait. Because increasing Black women's power and access would challenge the status quo of White male-dominated structures.

Like Tommy's story, Soya's situation shows how difficult it can be to hold more than one marginalized identity. Black women juggle the challenges of being in subordinated race *and* gender groups. According to a 2022 *Women in the Workplace* report, "Black women leaders are more likely to have colleagues question their competence and to be subjected to demeaning behavior" (Thomas et al. 2022, p. 17). This speaks to why 50 percent of women of color are thinking of quitting their jobs within the next two years (Barry 2020). Fed up with being passed up, overlooked, underpaid, and devalued, Black women professionals leave imposterizing work spaces to start new opportunities. Or they blaze their own trails and launch businesses. They do this in search of psychologically safer places that will recognize their worth, affirm their belonging, and foster their potential. This goes for any person, from any background, who feels imposterized in a space, and desires to transition to an uplifting environment.

Responding to Imposterizing Treatment

People who commit imposterizing acts can do so on purpose. But it's fair to admit, many others do so unknowingly. Even well-meaning folks can imposterize others. Biases about who belongs and who is deserving are so deeply ingrained in culture, it's almost second nature for people to value some groups of people more than others. However, it's everyone's charge to discard false narratives and treat all people as important, worthy, and capable. Each person has a part to play in dispelling harmful standards and redoing ideals we use as guides for living.

Leaders of groups, organizations, families, communities, and all other establishments are especially responsible for doing something about imposterizing practices. It's up to folks with decision-making power to dismantle oppressive structures. And it's their role to make spaces *consistently* welcoming of everyone involved. The power holders' job is to also eliminate prejudiced stamps of worthiness from rules and norms. In all, everyone has an important role to play in fixing imposterizing settings. But what can *you* do within your own personal power when you are imposterized? Here are some options.

Externalize the Problem

Ask yourself, *Is my environment supportive or oppressive?* In Soya's case, she went from self-assured to second-guessing herself. Her confidence was tampered with because of the setting she was in. So, before falling into the trap of self-blame, examine your surroundings. Remember this when you are disregarded, discriminated against, shunned, slighted, or unappreciated—it's not you who needs to be fixed. It's your environment.

Reduce Imposter Anxiety Through Compassion

Some folks are socialized to believe they belong in certain spaces solely because they represent a dominating identity group. Then they treat you like you're less-than to feel like they're better. But people who attempt to imposterize you, chances are they feel like frauds themselves. You're not obliged to internalize the negative messages these folks project on you. These toxic thought patterns are often what they are grappling with in their own minds—and that's their responsibility to address, not yours. But just as you show compassion to yourself in navigating self-doubt, I also encourage you to extend that same empathy to the folks who imposterize you. They may not deserve your generosity. But choosing kindness reveals your understanding that imposter anxiety manifests differently for everyone. Let me be clear. Being compassionate doesn't mean you let folks run all over you. So, in the parts to come, I'll show you how to confront imposterizing situations but to do it with care.

Prepare for Action

Being imposterized awakens the inner disrupter. But know this. Your survival instinct wouldn't activate the inner disrupter if your environment was an emotionally safe space. When the disrupter shows up, apply the seven steps from chapter 3 to respond to it. Prepare to also implement a set of actions to respond to the imposterizing setting you're in. That is, decide if you want to continue your involvement in that space or if you wish to end it.

SHOULD YOU STAY OR LEAVE?

As you contemplate your course of action, keep this imagery in mind. You live in a city where the air is heavily polluted. Being in that atmosphere is like smoking three packs of cigarettes a day. You exercise and eat nutritious foods. But no matter what you do to take care of your body, you're still in that toxic environment. You're constantly inhaling contaminated air into your lungs. This takes a toll on your health. You fall ill and the quality of your life is affected. The city's pollution is out of your control. But what you *do* have control over is whether you stay in that city or not. Being imposterized is like living in that hazardous climate. You are fully capable and worthy. But in your environment, you breathe in negative notions that infect your thoughts, feelings, and actions. You become emotionally sick. And in this case too, you can do something about it. You can choose to leave imposterizing atmospheres. Or you can remain in them.

Without a doubt, your decision may not be a simple one. And what you choose to do is valid no matter what you decide. Because all sorts of important factors will influence your chosen path. For instance, if you decide to leave, there's no guarantee that the next place you enter will be healthier. And factors like your finances are important to think about if the imposterizing space is also your source of income. Determine what's best for you at this point in your life by weighing the pros and cons of staying or exiting. And keep in mind, the self-doubt you experience from being imposterized could also influence your decision to leave or stay. Be able to identify this, and as mentioned before, use the guide from chapter 3 to respond to the inner disrupter.

CHOOSING TO STAY

Deciding to remain in spaces where you feel imposterized doesn't mean all hope is lost. You can try to improve your environment. One way is by "carefronting" (Kupperschmidt 2006) the people who imposterize you. You confront them with care. You raise your concerns as thoughtfully as you can. It can feel scary to speak about conflicts, because you worry about coming across as aggressive. But if your aim is to improve your experience, then carefronting could help you achieve this. Here's how to do it.

Be empathetic. You learned that people who imposterize you could be dealing with their own insecurities. Keeping this in mind enables you to approach your conversations with empathy. When you are empathetic, you're properly positioned to address others compassionately. Reacting aggressively can be avoided when your efforts are empathetic.

Be discerning. If a single person is imposterizing you, have a private conversation with that individual. Keep it one-to-one rather than confronting that person in front of others. Involving those who don't have anything to do with the situation could cause more harm than good. If it's a collective concern, though, you can raise the issue with your group. Workplaces will have their own protocol for responding to conflict. This may require you to speak with your supervisor about your concerns first before thinking of addressing an entire group of people.

Plan what you will say. Take time to think through your approach. And be clear and concise in describing your experience to the folks you're carefronting. Your goal is for your message to be understood, not lost in translation. Prepare solutions to your concerns and offer them to those you are addressing. Seek support from a professional, like a counselor or a coach, if you want to make sure your approach is solid.

CHOOSING TO LEAVE

If you've tried to rectify imposterizing situations, and you're unsatisfied with the outcome or you feel hopeless about the situation, your choice might be to leave. Figuring out your transition is your next point of action if you no longer intend to be in that environment. Consider creating a departure plan. Some situations don't need one—like, if they involve strangers who don't play any ongoing roles in your life. You can decide to leave without establishing an exit strategy in a case like that. But when there are important factors at stake, like your finances, handle those situations differently. Carefully plan how to make your leave as seamless as possible for you. Keep in mind, your plan may not pan out exactly as you want. But be sure it aligns with your values and that you handle it thoughtfully. Ask yourself these questions as you strategize:

- *Whom do I need to notify of my intention to leave?*

- *What do I need to have in place?* Do you need to have money saved up? If the setting is work related, do you need to have another job lined up?

- *What is my departure time line?*

Staying or leaving imposterizing situations is your decision to make. In the long run, aim to invest your time in empowering spaces instead of imposterizing ones. You deserve to be respected and treated like you belong.

You've learned how to address imposter anxiety when it's sparked by oppressive environments. In the next chapter, you'll explore how other external influences, like traumatic encounters, affect your experience with imposter anxiety.

CHAPTER 5

Affirm Your Awesomeness

Trauma is like a stone flung into a pond. The first splash is loud and strong. But the ripples continue after the stone has been thrown. What does that stone look like for you? In the moment, maybe you froze. Maybe you shed tears. Maybe you fled the scene. But long after the incident passed, the experience still reverberates in your life. You carry an unresolved wound without recognizing its detriment, as the toxic messages you absorbed taint your sense of self and prompt you to shrink, affecting your most important moments. The encounter happened in the past, so you think it's strong hold on you has dissolved. This is far from the truth. If emotional injuries from deeply cutting incidents remain unaddressed, the trauma continues to ripple through your life. But just as a pond eventually returns to stillness, healing, for you, is possible. You can settle the rippling effects of a trauma stone and stop the cycle of self-sabotage. The way to achieve this is to bring your past wounds to the forefront, unlearn negative narratives, and accept positive truths about your identity. Along the way, you'll gain new knowledge about your amazing qualities—the kind you'll feel empowered by to stand unshaken as the remarkable and worthy person you are. So, prepare to examine your emotional pain from the past. You'll likely discover underlying triggers of your experience with imposter anxiety when you do.

Traumatic encounters are deeply stressful events. The emotional harm they cause can bury itself deep in your soul, last for a long time, and show up strongly later in your life. Especially wounds from childhood incidents.

Because when you're a kid, you're impressionable. You're trying to understand who you are. And ideas you get from others, whether good or bad, become a staple in your mind. Especially when it comes from someone who matters to you. This was the case for me as a twelve-year old girl.

Before heading out with my sisters to get our hair done, Mommy gave me a twenty and told me to bring back the change. At the salon, I handed the stylist the bill. She explained some details I didn't understand. I nodded. And she gave me back a few dollars. I folded the bills and shoved them deep in my pocket without counting them. My only concern was to finally get my hair done. I was extremely excited to be sitting in a salon chair—not the dining room chair I always sat in for my oldest sister to do my hair at home, but in an actual salon—so I could get a trending style like the ones the girls at school wore. I depended on the adult stylist to do the math correctly and return the right amount of change. Apparently, I didn't bring back the total Mommy expected.

Sternly, she demanded, "Tell me the truth of what happened. Where's the rest of the change?" I had no idea how much the stylist handed back to me, so what was I going to tell her? "You are so stupid!" Mommy shouted. "Get out of my sight!" I quickly climbed the stairs and scurried back to my room. Over the coming days, Mommy let me know she was sick of my stupidity.

Confused and horrified, I was unsure of what to do. I knew I didn't lie. I wasn't trying to be mischievous. But I was, indeed, clueless about what happened with the money. I don't know why the returned amount was mismatched. I concluded, *If mommy is so mad at me, I must have done something really stupid. I must be really stupid. I...am stupid.* From then on, *stupid* was tattooed in my mind. It echoed again and again: *I am stupid. I am stupid.* I started believing I was born dumb and incapable of doing things right. Going to the salon for the first time in my life started off as a happy experience. But this exciting event did a 180 and became one of the most emotionally damaging days of my life—so harmful, I carried this notion of *stupid* with me to school, in my friendships, as I related to my siblings, when interviewing for jobs, at team meetings, and so on. It was the identity I subconsciously accepted as my truth for a long time.

Throughout my life, I rarely thought about that interaction with my mother. It wasn't until much later that I became fully mindful of how impactful that label was on me. The word "stupid" haunted me in moments when I wanted to participate or contribute but was hesitant to do so because I was afraid of being exposed as such. But the day I took a deep dive into my history to investigate this belief, I came to understand how that childhood incident had been a major source of my imposter anxiety.

You may think the pain from an early-life encounter is a thing of the past, without realizing these wounds can be buried and resurface when triggered. Maybe your parent said you weren't smart enough when your grades weren't all As. Now, every time you take an exam, you're convinced, *I'm going to fail.* Or your middle school teacher said you had poor writing skills. Now, whenever you prepare annual reports at work, you fret, *Will my boss think I'm a horrible writer?* Without starting the healing process, your emotional injuries will continue to feed your fears and self-doubt. It isn't your fault if someone hurled cruel words at you. But it's up to you to heal from those harms. I'll show you how.

Unlearn Negative Self-Beliefs

Don't spend another second living with an unhealed wound. If you're ready, reveal it to heal it. Start by finding ample, undisturbed time in solitude, holding space for yourself to be open and honest. With a paper and pen in tow, begin to unlearn negative self-beliefs with these steps.

1. Point out a toxic self-perception you internalized from a traumatic event.

2. Identify when it drives feelings of inadequacy in you.

3. Write about why this negative message is untrue.

4. Decide you won't accept that imposterizing narrative any longer.

As you move through these steps, pay attention to how your body responds. You may notice a visceral reaction within you, like sweaty palms, heaviness in your throat, or an ache in your gut. Your body reveals how much of a grip the self-limiting belief has on you. But as you follow the guides in this chapter, you can begin to free yourself from the stronghold of your past pains.

Have a Conversation

Earlier, I shared a story about my encounter with my mom to illustrate how traumatic events influence imposter anxiety. My mother has made more positive gestures in my life than anything else. But I also recognize how adultism (oppression of children) plagues parent-child relationships in ways we often don't see as problematic and traumatic for the child (Flasher 1978). I wanted to mend the emotional wounds my self-doubt was triggered by. So, I initiated a conversation with my mother to speak with her about my past hurt involving her. I needed to express how the incident made me feel and how it affected my life. You can consider this option too if you believe a conversation is an opportunity for you to reclaim your personal power and alleviate your pain.

It's not easy to initiate these kinds of talks. But here's what you can do to feel more confident in taking this step. First, give yourself a chance to acknowledge, feel, and validate your emotions. Then *prepare* for the conversation. You can enlist support from a mental health professional if you need help readying your mind for the chat. Also, spend time planning out your talking points. This is a good way to be sure you factor in what you wish to say. If you prefer not to speak, then consider writing a letter. When you decide to approach the person who catalyzed your emotional wound, let go of any expectation you have of them. Be clear on your own goals for connecting with that person, though. No matter the outcome of the conversation, find solace in knowing you took a bold step toward your healing. Also know that it's okay if you don't want to communicate with them about what happened. You might prefer to converse with a therapist about your past wounds, instead.

CHECKING IN   Do you wish to have a conversation about a past traumatic event? If so, with whom and when?

Reconsider Your "Weaknesses" as Strengths

You've learned to scrap false beliefs about yourself so you can replace them with positive truths. This is important to do. But also consider this. What if an attribute you think is a weakness or an embarrassing trait is actually your strength? You can see how this is true for Kyle, a kid whose classmates made fun of him for the way he delivered his presentation.

Story: Kyle

Gripping his well-typed essay, Kyle walked to the front of the room, facing about twenty staring eyes. Among them were the ones belonging to a menacing circle of boys. Our language arts teacher dipped her head, giving Kyle his signal to start. With his shoulders pulled back and head leveled, Kyle began. His voice was strong, enunciating every word clearly and maintaining a well-balanced pace. His declarations were moving, and his delivery, inspiring. Kyle was doing an outstanding job. He even managed to make gestures the rest of us weren't bold enough to do: to scan the class audience regularly while speaking.

When each of us had our turns, we dared not lift our heads when we spoke. That would be a death wish—like handing the group of boys an all-inclusive pass to laugh at you forever. Unlike the rest of us, Kyle did what he was supposed to do. He didn't bury his nose in his notes the way we did. Instead, he made frequent eye contact. Doing so was costly, though, because each time Kyle lifted his head to engage the crowd, the clique of boys burst into laughter. They laughed hard. But Kyle persisted. It was as if there was no other way for him. He was going to either reduce himself to avoid being made fun of or do what he knew to do. Kyle chose the latter.

His natural gift of gab was too grand to be stifled. The boys mocked him for being "weird." But what the boys deemed a turnoff is what many others view as talent. The irony of this story is the way things panned out for Kyle, because the quality he was belittled for is the same attribute he uses to flourish in his career today, earning a living by speaking boldly before a judge and withstanding the emotional rigors of legal cases. Kyle became an attorney. It's thrilling to know those boys' teasing points turned out to be Kyle's valuable assets. So be encouraged. What you perceived as a weakness could very well be your gift. Reconsider that "weakness" and regard it as your mighty strength.

CHECKING IN   How is a characteristic you're criticized for actually your strong suit? Like when someone says you're "too emotional" when you're simply an empathetic person. Or, like being accused of being "too quiet" when you're just a great listener.

Learn About Your Qualities

After you unlearn negative self-beliefs, fill your mind with constructive facts about who you are. Being aware of your good qualities helps to reprogram your beliefs and dispel those myths you accepted for far too long. Sure, the inner disrupter can show up again when triggered in certain situations— it'll try to steer you away from where you wish to be. But when you have knowledge of who you are in your toolbelt, you can use it to respond to the inner disrupter effectively. Soak up your positive attributes as you learn about them. Admire and appreciate them. And allow your awareness of your qualities to drive you in leaning into your goals. Start your learning process by taking time to realize your various traits, like your personality, abilities, interests, and the accolades you've garnered through your experiences. In each of these areas, what do you understand to be true about you?

Your Personality

You might view your personality as how you behave—like being outgoing or shy, or humorous or serious. Personality is that and more. It's also your unique combination of thoughts, emotions, and behaviors, which is shaped by your genes, your environment, and your experiences. All these factors work together to create the fascinating individual you are. How you interact with the world is influenced by your personality. And one personality type is not better than another. All types are important and meaningful in their own ways. Over time, your personality will constantly evolve. But consider this current point in time. Think about how you describe yours.

- Are you more on the verbally expressive side or are you inclined to process your thoughts internally?

- Do you gain energy by being around others or do you recharge by being alone?

- Do you like teamwork or would you rather work solo?

- Do you prefer structure or are you a spontaneous person?

Look at all four continuums in figure 2. Where would you place yourself on each of them?

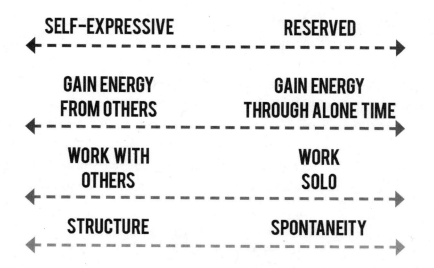

Figure 2: Personality Continuums

You can learn more about yourself through personality assessments. Many of these tools can be accessed online for free. Use them to gain more perspective on your qualities. Here are a couple:

- https://www.16personalities.com

- https://www.personalitymax.com

CHECKING IN   In your journal, write about where you placed yourself on all four continuums and why each of the ways you describe yourself is amazing.

Your Lived Experiences

You've lived through a lot. Happy moments, trying times, victories, losses. These experiences leave impressions in your mind, giving insight to what makes you, you. Your life story is what prolific storyteller Dennis Ross describes as "what happened because of what happened" (Ross 2022). That is, who you became because of what you experienced.

Your history is a great source of intel. You can spot out your qualities when you examine the events you've been through. But also consider starting new ventures to advance your journey of self-discovery, daring yourself to move beyond what you're familiar with to explore the unknown. Be intentional about meeting new people and trying different things. This way, you keep learning about yourself and come to appreciate who you are.

CHECKING IN   Think of an experience you wish to have that will help you expand your knowledge about yourself. Set a time line for when you will pursue it.

Your Talents and Gifts

Your talents are the things you're good at. They include what you know and what you can do—like being good with money, knowing how to use a particular software, or excelling at crafting. Your upbringing, hobbies, schooling, and work training are common talent-building experiences. When it comes to your talents, think of the skills you're mastering over time. What have you been acknowledged or rewarded for knowing or doing? What know-how distinguishes you from others? Check out this list of talents, adapted from *S.H.A.P.E.: Finding and Fulfilling Your Unique Purpose for Life* (Rees 2006). Which of them best describe you?

List of Talents

Analyzing	Managing
Collaborating	Negotiating
Communicating	Organizing
Computing	Performing
Connecting	Persevering
Constructing	Persuading
Cooking	Planning
Counseling	Promoting
Decorating	Recruiting
Designing	Repairing
Empowering	Researching
Engineering	Serving
Estimating	Shopping
Executing	Strategizing
Facilitating	Teaching
Guiding	Traveling
Landscaping	Visualizing
Leading	Writing
Learning	

Adapted from S.H.A.P.E. Finding & Fulfilling Your Unique Purpose for Life, Erik Rees © 2006

Your talents may not come naturally to you, but you have gifts that do. Your gifts are the qualities you don't have to work hard to develop. They are what others say make you special. But because they feel effortless, you may think they're not a big deal. Your gifting is your natural intelligence (Gardner 1983). Though they are nurtured by your environment, your gifts are part of your DNA. Your hard-wiring. You don't necessarily have to move outside of your comfort zone to excel at your gifts. And you feel like you're operating in your element when you embrace them. Your gifts are important and necessary functions to sustain humanity. Of the natural gifts listed, which of them best describe yours?

- *I'm good at visualizing objects from different angles.*

- *I'm good at understanding nature and living things.*

- *I'm good at discerning sounds and music.*

- *I'm good at understanding my thoughts, feelings, and behaviors.*

- *I'm good with words and speaking.*

- *I'm good at math and logic.*

- *I'm good at coordinating my body movement.*

- *I'm good at relating to and empowering others.*

- *I am deeply spiritual and in touch with the unseen.*

CHECKING IN   Using one to three of the descriptions as prompts, elaborate on the statements of your natural gifts. Describe your gifts in your own words, detailing what they look like in your life.

When you use your talents and gifts for altruistic purposes, you add value to any setting you're in. Knowing how valuable your qualities are to the world, you can stand confidently in who you are and boldly embrace these stand-out features of yours.

Your Interests and Passions

Your passions and interests are areas you get excited about more than other areas. You're curious about them. And they hold your attention and inspire you to be engaged in them. Thoughts about your interests and passions run through your mind more often than the average person. And they inform your goals and fuel your desire to offer solutions to needs you've identified in those areas.

> **CHECKING IN**   Pause and think of an interest that lights a fire in your heart. What issue do you feel pulled to solve? What group or audience are you motivated to support?

Learning about your good qualities is a lifetime endeavor. This is because you'll keep moving through new experiences throughout your life. And there are endless directions you can take to become more familiar with yourself. Some paths will be easy. Others will be more challenging. But by growing more acquainted with who you are each time, you gain an appreciation for yourself, making the effort well worth it.

Accept Positive Feedback

Imposter anxiety is a bizarre reaction. Notice how you can be distrusting of yourself when dealing with it. But at the same time, you have trust in negative views about yourself. That's quite the contradiction. If you don't trust yourself, then why believe the toxic notions about what you're capable of? Would it not make more sense to accept positive feedback others give you than to believe the self-limiting ideas in your mind?

Here's what accepting positive feedback can look like. First, reach out to others to learn what they have to say about you. Talk to trusted friends or family members, and ask them, "What qualities do you see in me?" It's a chance to gather new insights about your potential and your strengths, which can help you understand yourself better. The characteristics your feedback providers point out could also be qualities you have a hard time seeing on your own. Dare to trust their kind comments. Internalize those messages. Regard their words as affirmation of your awesomeness, indicating to you that you are making an impact. And allow this information to motivate you to embrace who you are and act more courageously.

Along with asking for feedback, accept compliments you didn't ask for. This information is also worthy of being internalized. But the challenge with this is accepting praises while dealing with self-doubt. Isn't it interesting that you want people to admire you, and you desire to be influential, but when folks express what they like about you, you feel like shriveling back or shying away from the praise? This can happen with any type of compliment—whether it's about your intelligence, personality, an accomplishment, or any other attribute. You might struggle with believing people's praises for a couple of reasons. One, you're unsure if you can keep up with the way they view you. And two, you measure your worthiness according to some arbitrary metric and you feel you haven't met the standard. I felt this way during my earlier years in college.

Total strangers approached me, saying "You're beautiful." This happened multiple times in a single day. Some with romantic agendas, some without. "You have a great smile." But I automatically felt awkward: *What do they see in me?* At the time, toxic beliefs about who was beautiful were deep-seated in my mind. People's praises didn't match what I felt about myself.

But picture this. A friend hands you a custom-designed, beautifully wrapped present, finished with a bow on top. What do you do with the gift? You accept it, of course. You stretch out your hands, take the present, exclaim, smile, and say, "Thank you." Now picture doing the opposite. Your friend gives you the gift. You push it away, shaking your head, and say, "Oh, no, I can't accept it." With the rejecting response, imagine the feelings it would elicit in the other person. Would they feel silly for giving you the gift? If they feel this way about their kind gesture, they probably won't do it again. Think of the act of brushing off your compliments in this way.

To be clear, the goal isn't to accept people's acknowledgements of you just to keep getting praises from them. Rather, it's about recognizing *compliments as gifts* when they come. They reveal the positive regard others have for you. And discounting them is like rejecting a thoughtful gift someone specifically handpicked for you.

It's hard for some people to give compliments. So, when you receive them, honor those verbal affirmations by showing gratitude for them. Your appreciation can motivate others to support you more and more. So, here's what to do. Imagine preparing a meal for someone, for example, and they say to you, "I love the way you cook." And your reply is, "Really? But…" This kind of reaction disregards the compliment. Instead, respond with a "Thank you, I appreciate it."

I challenge you, though, to take your gratitude a step further. Move beyond this basic response and give credit where credit is due. This means you say something like "Thank you, I appreciate it. I owe it to my dad, who taught me how to cook when I was ten. He would be happy to hear what you said." By adding a quick bit of background information, you showcase how meaningful the compliment is—with the giver and you as the receiver of the praise both gaining inspiration from your deeper reflection. Treat compliments like gifts. By accepting them, you invite more positivity and confidence in your life, as well as favor from others.

CHECKING IN   Write about your experiences with compliments. Why might it be difficult for you to accept them?

Affirm Yourself

Validation from others can be reinforcing. They are add-ons to support your understanding of yourself. But remember, validation from others is a cherry on top of a dessert—it's nice to have, but it's not necessary. In fact, depending too much on people's praises of you leads to insecurities (Cikanavicius 2017). You exert valuable energy wishing and wondering when someone will acknowledge you, so you can feel good for the moment. It's like pacing back and forth—tapping your foot over and over—waiting for a fleeting moment of validation. Relying on others to validate you gives them power to dictate your worth. Address this by finding a healthy medium. Accept external validation but do so without depending on it.

If you wait for people to see you, it becomes difficult to see yourself. Trust in your own understanding of your good features. Although affirmations from others can boost you up, your opinion of yourself matters more. Your ability to affirm yourself promotes a steadfast foundation within you, where you're unwavering about your awesomeness and optimistic about growing into an even more marvelous person.

Affirming yourself regularly is a good way to train your mind. I recognize, though, telling yourself *I got this* or *I can do it* can sometimes feel like fluff, or empty statements. So, make your words more substantive and evidence based. Do so by turning your affirmations into confirmations. For instance, if you declare *I am smart*, think of the many times you demonstrated your intellect. Do so by reflecting on your past accomplishments. This information is confirmation, or proof, of the positive things you say about yourself. Confirmations advance your affirmations, making your assertions more believable to you. Appendix A, "Imposter Anxiety Detox," is an affirmation meditation guide. There, you'll find a list of affirmations. Meditating on them will help to reinforce your awareness of how capable and worthy you are. Through this exercise, you'll also have a chance to turn those affirmations into confirmations.

CHECKING IN   Which of your good features would you like to be more mindful of? Write it out as an affirmation. Then confirm your affirmation by listing one to three reasons why it's true.

Archive Your Awesomeness

It's easy to overlook your positive qualities when dealing with imposter anxiety. But you can proactively address this. A useful approach is to write (Fritson 2008). Journaling is one form of this—where you record your thoughts and encounters—capturing your daily wins, big or small, as well as valuable lessons you learn each day. Journaling details the depth of your lived experiences. And when you revisit your entries, you can see your growth. This is when your capacity to achieve becomes apparent to you.

Samantha began journaling as a strategy for surmounting her self-doubt. As a rookie employee in a Fortune 500 company, she felt overwhelmingly incompetent in her role. She thought she didn't have much to offer to an organization full of high-performing, experienced professionals. Journaling daily was empowering to her because she started to see her worth and feel like a valuable member of her team. I encourage you to spend time journaling like Samantha did. It could be your ticket to greater self-awareness and appreciation for yourself.

Alongside journaling, consider another written form of archiving your awesomeness. You can keep a *success document*. Think of this as a one-or-two page, written (or typed) collection of your greatness, bullet by bullet. You might be surprised by how long your list gets. Unlike the narrative form of journaling, your success document is a list of all the good things about you. Create your own. And on it, write about the following:

- characteristics you admire about yourself
- your talents and gifts
- your potential
- your knowledge and skills
- your accomplishments
- your efforts
- compliments from others
- challenging experiences you overcame

Imposter anxiety makes it hard to recall your good attributes. But you can always go back to your success document when the inner disrupter shows up. Bring out your document when you need to get refocused. Create your own on a piece of paper, or you can keep an electronic version on file. Use any format you prefer and save it in a safe place. But even without whipping out your list, you might realize this: the visual memory of your success document—or the imagery of how long your list is—can be an ample reminder of how abundantly amazing you are. Journaling and keeping a success document are both useful ways to affirm yourself and remain sharply aware of your awesomeness.

In this chapter, you explored how past encounters shaped the toxic messages you internalized about yourself. You are now equipped to scrap your self-limiting beliefs by:

- unlearning negative narratives

- having a chat about your emotional wounds from the past

- reconsidering your weaknesses as strengths

- learning about your qualities

- accepting positive feedback from others

- affirming yourself

- documenting your amazingness

Healing from past wounds isn't achieved in a day. It must be practiced as a lifestyle, where you're working intentionally and on an ongoing basis to apply the strategies in this chapter. When you make these strides, you'll be well on your way toward moving beyond imposter anxiety and standing fully as the person you want to be.

You've seen how wounds from past experiences contribute to imposter anxiety. In the next chapter, I'll show you how to leverage your presence to address instances where you feel like you don't have much experience to be effective at what you do.

CHAPTER 6

Leverage Your Presence

Life is full of new experiences. And because they reveal your learning curves, starting them can feel scary. Think back to a time when you began something new. Especially those stages in your life when you didn't know much about what you were doing. Like being a first-year student, learning a different language, or becoming a debut novelist. How did you process those instances? Did you feel unprepared? Were you nervous about making a fool of yourself?

At the start of a new gig, navigating unfamiliar spaces, or when you're trying to get used to a certain lifestyle—these are all times when the inner disrupter emerges. You second-guess yourself. And you view your beginner status as a weakness. It's not your fault, though, if you feel self-conscious about what you're not accustomed to. Because society harps on rewarding people for their knowledge and experience. And when we believe we lack those qualities, we experience imposter anxiety. Our instincts then prompt us to prove our worthiness. But consider whether things might be different for you if you adopted a different mindset around limited experience. What if you viewed this status as a highly beneficial attribute?

Truth is, being new at—or in the early stages of—a role is good. These situations present opportunities to harness the power of your presence. You accomplish this by leveraging where you are in your growth. But this requires a deconditioning of your mind—to ditch the expectation of "having it all figured out"—so you can showcase the valuable qualities you currently possess.

One-year-olds come to mind when I think of beginners, because they have a lesser amount of know-how and life experience than adults. New to the world are these small humans. And unafraid of getting down and dirty are they as they explore their surroundings. They go about their merry way after making huge messes and are unbothered by how others view them. A fixation on perfection doesn't occupy their mental space. And they freely express their emotions. Expanding their bodies and their voices without reservation. Squealing with excitement, carefree about whose eardrums they're hurting. And smearing food all over their bodies to discover the sensation.

By nature, they show up unfiltered and in their full presence. This way of being allows them to explore their potential. And they build their awareness and skills in this mode. Toddlers don't hold as much knowledge as adults. Yet, with their limited experience, they manage to show their innate creativity and problem-solving abilities each day, demonstrating that even as beginners on this earth, they are capable.

And look at how we treat these little beings. We praise them even when they do things "incorrectly." And we think they are the most brilliant creatures in the world. Like a mother encouraging her toddler to say the word "carrot." The little girl says "cawwot," mispronouncing the word. Mom rejoices and shouts, "Good job!" And scoops her child up before landing tons of kisses on her face. Mom thinks her baby's errors are cute and celebrates her little girl for them. This openness from mom is good. It promotes a healthy space for her toddler to be her authentic self as she explores and learns.

But things change. The toddler is no longer that fully expressive child. She grows up; she's now an adult. Perfectionistic attitudes absorb deep into her mind as she starts to pick up on social norms around intelligence. She learns to conceal herself each time she starts something new. And she treads carefully when sharing her opinions, engaging in a reserved manner to avoid being judged or viewed as ignorant. Most of us have gone through a similar pattern in life. But this brings to question: Is toddlerhood the only time to relish in the newness of your experiences? Should it be the only point where you feel free to make mistakes? Is it the only period where you get to live without the fear of being seen as incompetent?

Sure, as you grow older, you'll have more responsibilities. And folks around you will expect more from you. But there will always be something new to learn. Is it worth it, then, to stress yourself trying to "know it all," especially when doing so drives imposter anxiety?

Here's what to do when you start new ventures or when you don't have much experience in an area. Believe in your ability to live your life unreservedly *and* responsibly. They can coexist. You can take on the free spirit of a toddler. And you can do so while applying wisdom in your moves. Question is, are you open to reclaiming the freedom you had as a tot? Be willing to return to a mind space where you're unashamed to express yourself. Where you embrace your curiosity and disregard opinions about how you *should* be. Toddlers thrive simply by being in their full presence. And you can, too.

The Advantage of Newness

People are inclined to associate a person's level of competence to their degree of exposure. But what does this mean for beginners if experience is what is readily favored by the masses?

You come with a clean slate, an eagerness to grow, and a fresh outlook on what could be, as a newbie. Your curiosity makes you inquisitive, and your questions can set new ideas in motion. Being a beginner is also a time to explore who you are and what you're capable of. You get to design your own story of how you started, so in the future you can see how you've evolved. There are many benefits of newness. A beginner status is just as essential as a seasoned rank. So, step into your full presence to explore and learn along your journey. There are advantages in doing so.

You Are Enough

Too often, we forget to leverage the qualities we already have. We reel over the skills or knowledge we're lacking. Then we end up feeling like we're not good enough. If this is the case for you, then I urge you to reexamine what it means to be enough. Does being enough mean you know more than your peers? Maybe it means you have at least five years of experience in an area. Or are you enough when you follow majority-ruled norms? Opinions around being *enough* differ for everyone. But not all definitions are accurate. Be cautious about defining your worthiness according to biased or limiting views. And embrace views that factor in your presence.

Here are healthy ways of understanding what being enough means. The urge to keep up with other people's standards is a nonfactor because you are content about what you bring. You accept and value where you are on your growth journey. You believe in your potential. You're confident in what you can do. But, to feel good about who you are, you must first *be* you: the authentic you, upholding your guiding values and doing what feels wise. You don't need to alter your personality to be enough. You are whole just as you are.

To be whole is to be complete. But don't confuse wholeness with perfection. Perfection is unattainable. And wholeness is something you already have. Perfection drives imposter anxiety. But embracing your wholeness fosters self-assurance. Wholeness shines a light on your true self: the parts of you that find serenity, joy, and confidence in your presence. You are whole, because within you is the possibility to become who you desire to be. You are whole, because you have all you need to get started on the life you want to live—like your current competencies and your natural strengths. You are whole because you are resourceful. You're constantly gathering new information and wisdom over time. And you can use this ongoing knowledge to inform your next steps.

Self-doubt arises, though, when you compare yourself to others. This is what makes you feel *unwhole*. You look down on yourself and assume, *I don't have enough exposure.* And you label yourself as having "limited experience." But don't be misled. Truth is, everyone has limited experience. Because no matter how familiar a person is with what they do, there will still be facets within their knowledge area that they have yet to explore. What you can experience in your life is without bounds. And the spectrum of know-how is endless. So rather than thinking you are inadequate, know you are more than enough. Embrace your wholeness through your presence. This is how to cultivate self-confidence.

Story: Melanie

Melanie was quiet in class. As for her peers, they spoke a lot. They shot their hands up in the air repeatedly, hoping for a chance to say their piece. When I called on them, their comments were well articulated. Melanie's approach was different. She barely spoke, but her presence stood out to me. It was her body language. Her attentive gaze, smiling face, and her open stance. Melanie's gestures signaled to me that she was engaged in her own way and curious to learn.

The students were enrolled in a leadership course I was teaching. This course was a chance to get to know students who were applying to be on staff in the residence halls. I facilitated group dialogues in this class, where I invited my students to share their perspectives on the topics being discussed. During each session, most of them spoke up to demonstrate how smart they were. They wanted to show me they were worthy hires. I appreciated the verbal participation of the outspoken ones. But little did they know, I was more intrigued by the one who barely uttered a word in class. The one who listened to her classmates speak and nodded her head to show her attentiveness. The one who positioned herself as a learner and took notes to capture the knowledge she was gaining. The one the other students probably thought would be the last person I would notice in a favorable way. The student who stood out to me was Melanie.

I appreciated her *presence*. She didn't contort herself to woo me with words. And her gestures gave me a sneak peek of her capacity to be a great leader and team player. Because of this, I grew eager to have Melanie on my staff. I valued her positive disposition more than whatever subject matter understanding or skill set she could have shown in class. Because I know a person's attitude determines their altitude.

My decision to invite Melanie to join my team was a good one. She turned out to be a top performer, a person adored by all her teammates, and someone whom I completely enjoyed working with. My hope for you is to recognize the power of your own presence. In many cases, your presence can hold more power than your competencies. You may not have all the expertise. You may not be the best speaker. You may not be the best performer. But through your presence, you can show up powerfully in any setting you're in. It's possible that Melanie's quiet nature in class could have been her reaction to feelings of inadequacy. Another probability is her disposition was her response to feeling centered and whole. Either way, the aspects of her presence she chose to showcase were the good parts. You can do the same, too, even when imposter anxiety strikes.

Presence and Performance

Your presence is the energy you put out into the world while your mind and body are engaged in an activity. Your mentality shapes your presence. And because of this, not all presence is the same. Presence is good. But there is also bad presence or, shall I say, disempowered presence—the type where you succumb to self-doubt and show those self-sabotaging behaviors of pushing back, escaping, shutting down, or people-pleasing. To counter imposter anxiety, harness your good presence. You'll learn how to do so in the parts to come. For now, let's distinguish *presence* from *performance*. Understanding their differences will help clarify how to focus your energy along your pursuit of the life you desire.

You've likely had an experience like this, where you read the qualifications for a role, then you say to yourself, *Forget about it, I don't meet the requirements.* You think you need all the skills listed before you can apply. But here's the issue with this thought: it places too much of an emphasis on your performance without considering the impact of your presence. The technical abilities you use to perform a task are only one contributor of presenting in a good way. But your presence is shown to be an even more valuable asset.

Mark Murphy, author of *Hiring for Attitude*, shed light on the importance of presence. In his 2017 book, Murphy wrote about his groundbreaking study where he reviewed twenty thousand new hires over a three-year period. What Murphy discovered through his research is a whopping 89 percent of the time new hires got in trouble or were fired was because of attitude, not skills. Your attitude *is* your presence. In Murphy's findings, attitude showed to be a more important factor than abilities. Knowledge and skills turned out to be unreliable predictors of how long new employees stayed in their respective organizations. What led to the new workers sustainability in their roles, though, was their positive attitudes or their good presence. Their success was rarely the result of their performance. From these findings, you can see how powerful presence is.

Don't get me wrong, presence and performance are both valuable. When done in a positive way, both qualities attract folks into your life. Both help you gain trust and favor from others. Both inspire people. But the misconception about performance still reigns in the minds of many, where people think their performance ability is the most important quality they can possess. But as Murphy revealed in his study, presence is often more meaningful than performance. Keep these findings on your radar as you explore how your experience with imposter anxiety is shaped by the way you perceive performance and presence. Which one promotes a healthy state of being when faced with self-doubt: pressuring yourself to perform perfectly or embracing your presence?

Again, the goal is not to minimize performance. Because your know-how is essential to the different roles you play. And aiming for quality in your performance is a way to make sure your tasks are done well. Notice, though, how the pressure to perform your responsibilities flawlessly, or focusing too much on showing good skills, sparks self-doubt. An overfocus on performance drives you to worry about doing things right so others can deem you worthy. But with presence, you don't need to have any special knowledge or talent. Your only requirement is to be authentically present.

I point you in the direction of your presence because by leaning into it you can mitigate imposter anxiety. In your presence, you show up as you are. You get to be true to yourself and explore your curiosity. You get to be a learner. And showing good presence is what allows others to connect with you on an emotional level. This connection motivates people to support you in reaching your goals or link you to promising opportunities you never imagined for yourself. On the other hand, worrying too much about your performance is like spinning on a hamster wheel. Whirling around a circle of never feeling like you're enough. But when you embrace your presence, you see what you have as sufficient. And your attitude and actions reflect your appreciation for the experiences you're having.

CHECKING IN   In what ways would you like to enhance your presence?

How to Be Present

Whether you're reaching for a milestone or honing your skills, you can rely on your presence. It holds a lot of influence in introducing you as an asset in any space. Question is, will you trust it to help you discover, learn, and evolve along the way? You are now sharply aware of what presence is. You understand its power. But now, it's time to learn how to leverage it. These seven steps will guide you.

1. Practice Mindfulness

To be mindful is to be present in the moment. You are aware of your thoughts and feelings without judging yourself. Like your response when the inner disrupter shows up. You acknowledge that it's there, and you interpret it as a reminder of the growth path you're on. When you're mindful, you're also intentional about your breathing. This is important because imposter anxiety is generated by perceived threats. And when you feel a threat, your reaction is to hold your breath. But did you know, deep breaths signal to your brain that you are safe? Breath work can help you reduce your chances of reacting with self-sabotage. So, when you feel the stress of self-doubt, redirect your attention on your breath. Notice the rise and fall of your chest, the sensation of air entering and leaving your lungs. The inner disrupter fades into the background as you focus on the here and now. Breathing in an appreciation of the lessons from your experiences. And breathing out anxiety and worry. This will anchor you in the moment and allow good presence to come through.

2. Acknowledge Your Status

It was my first week as a doctoral student when one of my outspoken classmates, Owen, exposed the elephant in the room: "Let's just go ahead and say what we're all feeling. We probably all feel like imposters right now." Everyone chuckled. His comment broke the ice. He called out the insecurity we were all experiencing as new faces in the program. We put our guards down after realizing we were all in the same boat, navigating the uncertainties of what was expected of us as PhD students, and trying to prove we belonged. After Owen's comment, I felt emboldened to be more authentic, open, and explorative with my classmates. I also stopped worrying about how they would judge me if I asked a question or shared my ideas. As you move through new experiences, I invite you to gracefully call out the elephant in the room. Disrupt the cycle of silence that can keep you stuck in self-doubt. And acknowledge the early phase of your growth journey.

Pointing out your current standing can help you bypass the shame being quiet about your status breeds.

There's a lot you won't know when you're new at something. And that's okay. You can still confidently stand in your truth. Here are some examples. Imagine someone asking you a question you don't know the answer to. Would you say, "Oh, I'm not sure," and feel embarrassed for not knowing? Or would you take your best guess and state it as if it were a fact, just to appear as though you know the answer? You don't have to do any of these. Instead, you can say something like "I appreciate your question. I don't know, but I'm happy to learn about it."

Consider this other scenario. You're expected to complete a task you haven't had much exposure in. A good response is to admit where you are now, then declare where you aspire to be. Like the popular saying states, "Speak what you seek until you see what you said." This brings your vision into your purview and clarifies what you're aiming for. Clarity on where you're heading helps boost your confidence about your growth process. You can also offer your support in work you either have more experience in or are more interested in. This means you say something like "I'm not quite experienced in this area, but I do know a lot about [related task you're familiar with] and can offer some ideas around [area you like that is related to given task]." With these communication strategies, you disclose your status on your journey while showing confidence and a willingness to learn and contribute.

3. Be Optimistic

"You're up," her professor said. It was Tessa's turn to take front and center. This was Tessa's first speaking assignment in law school. Throughout her presentation, she fumbled over her words and jumbled terminology. On top of that, she struggled with the audiovisual equipment. A wrinkle formed between her professor's brows. He clenched his lips tightly. Leaning back into his chair, his arms folded as he subtly shook his head from left to right. Tessa made her last statement, then gazed over at the professor, waiting to receive feedback. The professor released an audible sigh. A long silence followed. And before the class, he announced, "What was that? Do you realize how incomprehensible that was?"

Tessa could have frozen up after her professor's reaction. She could have wallowed in embarrassment. She could have seen herself as an imposter. And if she reacted in all these ways, it would be normal and understandable. But her response made her out to be quite the opposite of a fraud. Because to her professor, she gleefully replied, "I know. One day, I'll look back at this moment and see how far I've come."

He intended to disgrace her. But his gesture was like a boomerang. What her professor didn't know was this: Tessa viewed her challenges as learning opportunities. What he had employed as a mark of shame was what Tessa turned into a moment of inspiration. His criticism of her was what Tessa used to activate her sense of resolve. She acknowledged her early stage as a learner and expressed confidence about her future. She so gracefully disarmed her professor simply through her *optimism*. Tessa's classmates' faces lit up like sunshine. Some nodded their heads in agreement with her comment. As for the professor, he dissolved his grimacing gaze. His face turned red. Stumped by Tessa's response, he mustered up some final words, but this time, in a softer tone of voice. Can you see how Tessa's optimistic outlook defused an interaction that could have otherwise brought about imposter anxiety?

In life, you'll face situations where you're still learning the ropes. You'll question your ability to do the work. But recall past times when you eventually got used to your role after you initially felt like you had no clue what you were doing. What does this tell you about what you're capable of? Improvement is possible as time progresses. You are exactly where you need to be. Your optimism puts things in the right perspective. You view your experiences from your vision point instead of your vantage point. Focusing on the vision you have for yourself, rather than feeling small because of where you are now. Like Tessa, will you be optimistic when you start new ventures?

4. Be Prepared

Put together the things you need to feel more confident. Will you need a quick pep talk from a friend? Or does this mean you watch an empowering YouTube video before plunging into a new undertaking? Ready your mind and arrange the resources you need to feel equipped. For group settings, think about what could be helpful to the folks you're involved with. Would it benefit the group if you came up with ideas ahead of time? Or maybe you plan to pay attention to their nonverbal cues to anticipate any unspoken needs. Your awareness of potential needs equips you to explore them proactively.

Being prepared is also about being punctual and ready to give your best, demonstrating your respect for others and their time. Also, prepare for the unpredictable by being open to change. Things may not pan out the way you want, and that's okay. Allow what you plan for to take you as far as it can. Then, for the rest of your experience, be flexible with what happens. Because in everything—whether you're readying your mind for a date, a delicate chat with a friend, an important neighborhood meeting, or any other activity—there is a learning opportunity.

5. Show a Willingness to Participate

Show your willingness through your body language, paying attention to the messages you send through your gestures. Demonstrate your interest through eye contact, nodding occasionally, and maintaining an attentive posture. You can also actively participate by talking *and* listening. Both forms of engagement are powerful. But you might be inclined to speak a lot to be seen as smart. Be aware of this pressure and dismiss it. You don't have to be talkative to have an impact. Making concise comments or holding space for others to speak is also influential. Volunteering or taking initiative is another way to express your willingness to engage. But as you give your time and energy, listen to your body and be sure to take care of yourself. Avoid overwhelm by striking a good balance in how involved you get.

6. Be Open to Growth

Recall those moments when you were in a room full of people you thought were smarter than you. How did you feel? For many, they felt like hiding. It's easy to assume *I'm not supposed to be here*. But how does being the most knowledgeable person in a room help you grow? If you're the smartest person there, then you've outgrown the space. You get to expand your brainpower when you're around folks who have arrived at stages you want to reach. And if you're not in the company of folks who know more than you, then it's time to reconsider the environments you're in. Join spaces where you can be stretched. When you're surrounded by people who can take your learning to the next level, you're exactly where you're supposed to be.

7. Replace Apologies with Empathy and Gratitude

Do you find yourself apologizing for not having as much know-how as others? Thinking your newness is an annoyance to others can prompt you to overapologize. You say "sorry" over and over because you feel guilty for taking up sought-after space. Overapologizing is a people-pleasing reaction. Be unapologetic about your newness. There's no need to tell people "I'm sorry" for what you haven't been exposed to or what you don't know yet. Or for things you can't control. Or for not having all the answers. Or for requesting help. Don't waste your time lamenting what you don't have. Pull from what you *do* have. Like your presence.

Replace apologies with exclamations about what's to come. Do this by saying things like

"I'm excited to…"

"I'm ready to…"

"I'm eager to…"

Rather than saying sorry for things that aren't your fault, make empathetic statements to be considerate of the other person's thoughts and feelings. Being empathetic involves putting yourself in the shoes of another person. So, you can say something like "I understand you need the information tomorrow, so you can finish your assignment." You can also show gratitude when responding to others. Gratitude is about being appreciative of the other person. So, instead of saying "Sorry for bothering you," say "Thank you for helping me." It's okay to take up space as you explore new experiences and learn. In all, be mindful about overapologizing when you haven't done anything wrong. And swap apologies out with empathy and gratitude.

CHECKING IN Name a setting where you plan to lean into your presence more. What does doing so look like for you?

I invite you to discover the opportunities that your new experiences offer. As you enter them, remember: your newness is valuable, and your presence is enough. Practice mindfulness. And be optimistic, open, prepared, and willing to participate. Leveraging your presence in these ways will help you respond well when you face imposter anxiety: showing up positively and in the truest ways you can.

A powerful way to be present is to revel in what makes you different. In the next chapter, you'll learn how to delight in your difference to move past imposter anxiety.

CHAPTER 7

Delight in Your Difference

Immigrating to the United States at age four, I knew I was different. My teachers struggled with pronouncing my Nigerian name. Especially on the first days of school when they took attendance. I knew my name was coming up because the teachers would always pause, take a breath, and say, "Oh, boy, this is a tough one," or "Forgive me for butchering this name," or "I know I'm saying this wrong, but…" Sometimes, while they were giving their preface, I'd go ahead and raise my hand and say, "Here." I thought, *Let me save them the trouble.* Each shot they took at pronouncing my name was a constant reminder, *I have a difficult name. I am different.*

When was the first time you noticed your difference? Perhaps it was on a sports team or when you were playing outside with the other neighborhood kids. When you recognized this, what do you remember about that moment? Teachers slaughtering my name was one realization of my difference. But a more poignant encounter happened on my high school gym floor. My difference became not only widely apparent to me then but also a source of my imposter anxiety.

When Ms. Duncan announced I was to be the season's cheer captain, her smile stretched widely. I was surprised. *Who me?* I had no idea this could happen. But I was ecstatic it did. Some girls clapped. A few shouted a quick "Whoo-hoo." And from several others, I received hugs and pats on my back. Everyone was excited for me. Or so I thought. My cloud nine moment suddenly turned into a cloudburst of confusion. Three of the cheerleaders glared at me with their eyes signaling disbelief and disapproval. They huddled together in what looked like a rigid U-shape with their leader gazing at me with her arms folded. Her face resembled the look you give after sniffing a bottle of expired milk.

Questions swirled in my mind about their reaction, but nothing seemed to make sense. So, my fourteen-year-old brain was left to compare physical differences. The three girls were White. I'm Black. *Maybe they think I'm not supposed to be captain because I'm Black.* It was the main difference I could glean at the time. My confusion turned to self-consciousness. The subtle messages I picked up about my difference affected the way I felt about my belonging in majority White spaces. This was one of my struggles throughout high school and into my early twenties.

By learning facts about difference, I turned self-limiting perceptions around for myself. I'll give you insights to delight in the splendor of your difference throughout this chapter. But first, be clear on what is meant by *difference.* Everyone is born different. And there are a variety of ways to be different. Your difference could come from your physical attributes, like the color of your skin and your height. Differences can be mental, like your natural intelligences or your temperament. They can also be spiritual, like your belief in a higher power or your understanding of the universe. Your social identity, choices, and circumstances can make you different, too. Whatever your differences are, your distinct features set you apart from others. And they are, therefore, what make you special.

Is Difference an Advantage or Disadvantage?

Geckos have the amazing ability to camouflage their bodies. They generally go completely unnoticed. But once they feel their cover is blown, they begin to show signs of stress. How familiar does this experience of vulnerability sound to you, where you feel exposed because of your difference? You may feel this way when you're one of the few of your kind in a space. So, like the gecko, you blend in to feel safe, hiding the real you. You recognize the implications if you don't disguise—to you, it would mean your lack of belonging is revealed. In your life, you may think you don't belong in some settings because of your difference.

But your difference is the very reason you belong. It's what makes you necessary. But despite the importance your difference holds, it's a source of shame for you. It's the reason you shrink back in certain situations. It's what sparks self-doubt. So, this leaves you wondering, *If my differences are supposed to be beneficial, then why do they feel like detriments?*

Your Unique Edge

You can guess what happens when everyone in a group is the same. Like when people are from the same background, share the same way of thinking, have the same gender or racial identity, or are in the same age group. Wouldn't they risk putting together the *same* sorts of ideas over and over? In the absence of difference, novelty and progress are at risk (Licalzi and Surucu 2012). Croitoru and his colleagues' 2022 study on diversity in the workplace confirmed this. Their research revealed the power of difference when it's leveraged properly. For example, when people who think differently get together, their efforts are more creative and innovative (Phillips 2014). This also makes what they produce more seamless and appealing to a variety of people.

So, next time you feel like the odd man out, recognize the value you add when you grace a group with your presence. Being different can be uncomfortable at times. Ideally, you would be in a diverse space where enough folks who are similar to you are present, so you don't feel overwhelmingly outnumbered. But when you're the only one of your kind, remember what you contribute. You could be the reason mundane efforts become more dynamic. When you offer your perspectives, you give others a chance to look beyond what they've typically seen. And you can bring more out-of-the-box ideas to the table. This wouldn't require you to gain any new kind of intelligence. Your unique qualities are valuable on their own. So, you see, your difference is not a disadvantage. It's your advantage. It's your unique edge and it's worth relishing.

The "Other"

Being different can feel like you're an outsider, especially when folks you share commonalities with are absent. You see yourself as the "other," like Bridget did. Because of her accent, she felt out of place around her team. Bridget is from Alabama, and she took a job in Boston, moving states away to work in her dream job. Nearly all her colleagues were from Northeastern states. Bridget is the only one from the South. During her first team meeting, she immediately noticed how different she sounded. This dissuaded her from speaking up around them. If you've ever worried about people judging you because of a noticeable attribute of yours, then you can understand Bridget's situation. "I don't want them to look down on me because of my accent," she said. Her awareness of the negative stereotypes about people with Southern accents intimidated her. Being viewed as "soft" or "slow-witted" was a threat in Bridget's mind. So, she kept quiet. What Bridget experienced is known as a *stereotype threat*. This is when you are overly conscious about confirming stereotypes about your identity (Baysu and Phalet 2019).

Stereotype threat disrupts how you show up in spaces. Like a woman who is taking a math exam in a room full of men: *Women are not as good at math as men* is the stereotype she's grappling with. This thought affects her performance on the test—a test she would have done well on if a stereotype threat hadn't interrupted her focus.

Although stereotypes are inaccurate, these notions are widely spread across the world and even accepted in many cases. They feed the assumptions people make about different groups. So, it's understandable if stereotypes feel like threats to you. But here's how to address a stereotype threat. First, know you are not a stereotype. And remember the truth about who you are. You strip away interesting, good, and vital parts of who you are by giving the stigma of stereotypes space to govern your actions. Instead, use the tools I offer later in this chapter to shift your attention away from those false ideas and zero in on the advantages your difference brings—there are plenty of them.

CHECKING IN   What stereotypes do you feel threatened by? How do you react when you experience these predicaments?

Social Norms and Expectations

You can experience imposter anxiety when you think you don't live up to society's norms or expectations. Like the tall guy whose sport is chess. "You play basketball, right?" People he meets for the first time ask him this question. It happens often, and it sets his fraudulent feelings in motion. He loves chess and has no interest in shooting layups for a living. Or the woman who works in pipeline construction. She feels like the black sheep in her family when they talk about her career choice. A more "ladylike" career is what they believe she should have pursued. People tend to use norms as a metric for judging themselves and others. But do you use societal standards to determine if you are normal or not? Norms are a widely accepted set of ideas, rules, and actions within a society. When you don't fit norms, you may feel abnormal in certain spaces.

Social norms and expectations are used as a blueprint, shaping the environments you're in, like the workplace, where these ideas are woven into policies, procedures, and community standards—and where an ideal like *professionalism* is preached. Professionalism is about following the norms of an organization or other structured settings. Sounds ethical and seemingly sensible, right? The universal *do no harm* values of professionalism can be helpful.

But be mindful: many other aspects of professionalism can be imposterizing to you. Some of the principles of professionalism are actually *preferences* of the folks who shape the rules of the spaces you're in. And these preferences may not be fair to you. Because the rules of professionalism often fall short in factoring in difference. For example, professionalism includes rules around hair. A workplace may frown upon pink hair color or deem locs (also known as dreadlocks) as unprofessional. But the last time I checked, optimism, curiosity, knowledge, skills, and commitment contribute to a person's effectiveness at work. Locs and pink hair have nothing to do with how good of an employee you are. So why should these inconsequential, though beautiful, features of a person be used to determine whether you're professional or not?

CHECKING IN   How have social norms influenced the way you think of your difference?

"I want to show confidence, command the room, and carry myself like a leader," said Rachel, who is an aspiring executive professional. She sees men as examples of people with executive presence. Society does the same, too, often linking executive presence and leadership to qualities found in men. What Rachel imagines to be leadership presence may be one form of it. But it's not the only one. More importantly, it's certainly not a standard all people must follow.

Without the pressure to mirror societal opinions about leadership presence, here are some better ways to think of yours. Leadership presence is not about morphing into something you're not. Rather, it's about bringing forth the genuine and unique parts of yourself. You then inspire others to do the same. Leadership presence comes from trusting your difference and leveraging it.

Rachel already has true leadership presence—a nurturing nature, a collaborative spirit, and a supportive approach with her team. She needs to identify and cherish these qualities and believe in their power to position herself for the right opportunities. Achieving the type of leadership presence Rachel imagined she needed to have might or might not get her promoted. But let's say Rachel attains her desired position. Would her new role empower her to openly express her unique qualities, or would she still feel the need to keep up a simulation of who she thinks she needs to be? You may relate to the burden of presenting in ways you hope will win you favor, especially when you're doing your best to keep your head above water in certain spaces. This is a valid concern. But think about whether it's worthwhile for you to mold yourself into another person's ideas of leadership presence or if you're willing to embrace the special qualities you hold right now.

> **CHECKING IN**   What unique attributes do you appreciate about yourself? These features are essential to your leadership presence.

Social Capital

For the longest time, I wasn't aware of the word "charcuterie." Today, people use the word to describe wooden boards consisting of a variety of meats, nuts, vegetables, cheeses, artisan breads, crackers, and dips. I've certainly enjoyed these sorts of spreads in my life. But within my upbringing, I had no idea of its official name. Imagine if I was at a networking soiree in my earlier adult years, and someone asked me about the charcuterie spread. While I probably would have taken a guess at what they were talking about, I would not have known exactly what they were referring to. If I was worried about making a good impression, I probably would feel embarrassed.

Here is what's important to remember, though. Not everyone has the same kind of exposure. You'll be familiar with things others aren't knowledgeable of—and vice versa—voluntarily or not. Either way, your unfamiliarity with what someone else knows doesn't mean you're inferior. Your upbringing was just unlike theirs. And you, therefore, have a different set of *social capital*.

Social capital has to do with assets or qualities you have that benefit you in social settings (Bourdieu 1986). The way you were brought up, your lived experiences, and your social network influence the kind of social capital you have. The way you speak, the words you use, your approach to life, your interpersonal skills, and your cultural knowledge also make up your social capital. When you think you don't share the same social capital as the folks around you, you might feel unequipped to maneuver through spaces the way others move. Like when your interpersonal style is different from others. If you're more of a listener than a talker, for instance, and you're in a group full of conversationalists, you may assume you don't have the right kind of social capital to interact with them. Communicating verbally is essential for chats. But so is your ability to hold space for others by listening. Your ability to lend a listening ear is a quality people appreciate and respect, because it allows them to feel seen and heard. So, you see, both listener and talker approaches are influential. Both forms of social capital are valuable.

In all, the social capital you've gained through your culture, values, lifestyle, talents, and ideas are just as important as anyone else's. Your difference is what provides a healthy variety in a space. Don't discredit the power of your difference by assuming you lack social capital or don't have the right type. You simply have a different, and worthy, set of capital.

> **CHECKING IN**   How is your social capital different in the various settings you're in? I challenge you to use it to expose others to new approaches.

Your Difference Is Your Superpower

If you still think what makes you different limits you, then answer this. How does a person who is visually impaired win a cooking competition? On the show *MasterChef*, contestant Christine Ha's pie was the last to be tasted before the judges determined who would be eliminated from the contest. As Christine approached the panel, show host Gordon Ramsey asked Christine what she thinks her pie looks like. "I think it probably looks like a pile of rubbish," Christine responded. But it was the opposite: the top was perfectly crisp, it had no soggy spots, and the flavor was absolutely delicious. Christine went on to win the entire Season 3 MasterChef competition, becoming the first blind competitor of the series and the first contestant with a visual impairment to win the MasterChef title.

In an interview with *Mashed*, Christine said winning the pie contest was a confidence boost for her after she had experienced self-doubt during the competition (Allen 2021). Before her win, she assumed she was the worst cook since she couldn't see her opponents in action to tell if they were skilled or not. Christine's blindness didn't limit her from succeeding, though. During her conversation with *Mashed*, she pointed out folks' overdependence on their eyesight and how it deters them from tapping into their other senses. She spoke about her reliance on her other senses to cook, and she revealed her ability to taste the details in foods in more advanced ways than someone who is not visually impaired could. The main takeaway here is this: Rather than viewing your difference as a deficiency, see yourself as *differently abled*. We all are. What you think you're missing is instead an opportunity to activate other mighty parts of you. And when you do, you'll be well on your way to achieving your big dreams.

> **CHECKING IN**   How do your unique attributes allow you to do things differently, and maybe even more powerfully, than others?

How to Delight in Your Difference

Here's your chance to bring all the gems you gained about *difference* together. Apply these five steps to be more deliberate about embracing your distinct attributes.

1. Point Out Your Difference

No one else in this world has your exact set of experiences, characteristics, and DNA. Because you are one of a kind, you are truly a treasure. Take a moment to ask yourself, *What makes me unique?* Write down all the ways you feel different when around others, and spot the social capital you hold in your spaces.

2. Identify the Importance of Your Difference

Let's say you're looking to build a house. What would you rather have? A great painter and an even better painter? Or a great painter and a great interior designer? You'll likely choose the second option: to have workers who perform different tasks. If two of the same are present, then one of them may not be needed. Consider this, too. Imposter anxiety can have you thinking you need to be better than the next person to be worthy. But the real value lies in being genuine about what makes you *different*. The next step after identifying your unique characteristics is to write about why they are essential and worthy. Pick a setting where you are aware of your difference and use the following prompt. *I am needed here because* _____.

3. Cherish Others' Differences

Notice the distinct qualities of others and celebrate them for it. When you do this, you reinforce a culture of appreciation for diversity. This allows you to believe in and internalize the value of difference even more.

4. Use Your Difference for Good

Your unique makeup informs your life's purpose. So, use it to fulfill what you were designed to do. If you care about doing your part to improve the world, then make it your responsibility to leverage your difference. Tell others about your standout features, and communicate how your unique qualities can be used to help in a situation. Don't hesitate to offer up your one-of-a-kind insights, lived experiences, and attributes. Because there are people out there waiting for you to show up as you are, so they can live out their life purpose too.

5. Choose Authenticity

I admit, it gets hard to delight in your difference when influences like stereotypes, societal norms, social capital, and being the "other" in a space affect how you act. But I encourage you to show up the way you wish to be even if it means you deviate from the norm. Because attempting to fit in is like true fraudulent behavior—you're trying to conform to a way of life that is disingenuous to the real you. Being your genuine self moves you away from self-restricting ways of being. It allows you to experience a more liberated lifestyle.

But it's critical to know this: being authentic may be unfavorable in some settings. Not because your difference isn't worthy but because not everyone will appreciate diversity. This is Jodi-Ann Burey's argument in her 2020 TEDxSeattle Talk titled, "Why You Should Not Bring Your Authentic Self to Work." In her talk, Burey described how bringing your full, authentic self is proven to be "too risky." She explained how being your true self can yield the opposite of what you expect—meaning you open yourself up to be authentic, but the folks around you are unaccepting of your genuine self-expression. In such environments, being your authentic self usually privileges those who are part of dominating groups while disadvantaging those in marginalized groups.

Can you see how being authentic *in the wrong places* can further invoke imposter anxiety, especially if your identity is underrepresented in those settings? In chapter 4, I provided tips to consider when deciding your future in imposterizing spaces. Revisit those pointers if you're looking for steps to address these situations. You have a choice, though. You could either dwell in a space that welcomes you just as you are, or not. With only one life to live, will you choose authenticity?

CHECKING IN   Decide who you want to be in the spaces you're involved in. Ask yourself: *What parts of me would I like to express in this setting?*

To overcome imposter anxiety, accept your differences as your unique edge. The more you embrace your differences, the more your confidence will rise. Delighting in your difference isn't about *trying* to be different. It's about leaning into who you are today. Your path to freedom from the chains of societal norms is yours to tread. So, boldly welcome your one-of-a-kind qualities with open arms. And use them to build a life that reflects your true identity.

Embracing your differences correctly will require you to keep the ego in check. I'll show you how in the next chapter. And you'll learn steps to disarm the ego as a means for addressing imposter anxiety.

CHAPTER 8

Check the Ego

When I met Iris through a small community of women, I imagined forming a friendship with her, because I admired her a lot and we have a lot in common. But I noticed the difference between the way she treated me and our mutual acquaintances. She was exceedingly warm and welcoming to them. But Iris didn't extend the same level of energy to me. I thought, *What do they have that I don't?* Sure, she would hit the heart button on my social media posts. But I expected more. I tried to forge a bond with Iris. I attempted to dive deeper in our chats. But my efforts weren't necessarily reciprocated. I determined, *If Iris doesn't consider me the way she does with others, then I must be so uncool.* The difference in treatment was more than just a disappointment to me. It felt like a threat. A threat to my identity. A threat to my sense of self. But why did I feel this way?

The Ego

Earlier, you learned that the inner disrupter attempts to shield you from emotional harm. But when your instincts detect a threat to your sense of self, the inner disrupter turns to a particular entity living in you that guards your self-image. This force is the *ego*. Just as the inner disrupter is separate from the real you, so is the ego. The ego is not who you truly are (Kristina 2020). It's only a mechanism made up of a bunch of toxic ideas about what you deserve, how significant you are, and who you need to be to be loved and accepted. As for my situation with Iris, I wanted to be cool enough to be her friend. It's normal to want close connections, but the hitch lay in the thoughts I had about myself while I had these desires. Iris's approach with me was not the real problem—her actions may not even have had anything to do with me. The real issue was allowing the ego to shape my outlook of myself and giving it space to spark self-doubt in me.

Is Ego the Enemy?

Ego is natural. But so is asbestos, arsenic, and snake venom. Not all natural things are good for you. The ego becomes problematic when it's left unchecked. It gives rise to imposter anxiety, affecting how you think, feel, and act. It feeds your mind with perfectionistic expectations about who you ought to be. And because the ego always aims for you to be seen in a favorable way, it wants you to do anything to achieve this. Even if it means being inauthentic or changing parts of yourself.

The ego affects how you interpret feedback. Like an employee who feels offended by her boss who gave her constructive criticism during her performance evaluation. It leads you to play the victim—blaming others for outcomes you don't want attributed to you—and projecting your negative feelings about yourself onto others. With your focus only on your self-image, an ongoing frustration of never feeling like you're enough becomes a daily grapple. This drives you to lose sight of the greater purpose of your doings.

Ego is dangerous. It can send you down a dark hole of doubt, to the point of self-destruction. For Andrew Gillum, 32,000 votes was the trigger. This number changed his life forever. As a history making leader, Gillum became the first African American to be elected as the democratic nominee for Florida governor. But he wasn't victorious. Losing by 0.04 percent. That's 32,000 votes to be exact. He was close to winning. But he didn't. Sixteen months later, police found the same promising politician naked and passed-out drunk on a hotel bathroom floor—propped on his side, with his head lying on a pillow soiled by his own vomit. This scene became a scandal.

Photos of him blacked out and exposed on the bathroom floor had circulated. And commenters on Twitter had a field day with it. How did a figure who was endorsed by President Barack Obama get to this point?

On the *Tamron Hall* show in 2020, Gillum spoke about how he underestimated the way losing the gubernatorial race would affect his life. Andrew turned to alcohol, describing it as his "aide" to numb the shame he felt from not living the life he imagined he and his family should be living. People's opinions of Andrew triggered his suicidal thoughts; these thoughts were sparked not because of his reckless drinking behavior but because of people's criticisms of him. After the election, Andrew felt like he was "not on mission" and "not being purposeful." He described how he was giving speeches to people, telling them "You are enough," all while thinking to himself, *I'm a fraud.*

Andrew has since sought support through rehab and therapy. But consider this. Where would Andrew be today if he had recognized earlier on what an unchecked ego could lead to? What if he interpreted his election setback as an opportunity for something new? What if he viewed his potential beyond the governor title and kept his eyes on the greater purpose of his work? You have the chance to recognize all this now. So, as you encounter ego thoughts, remain mindful of the ruin it can cause if left unchecked.

With all the ways an unchecked ego is detrimental, you can see the accuracy in the title of the book *Ego Is the Enemy* by Ryan Holiday (2016). As you learned earlier, people can imposterize you. But with the ego, you have an imposterizing agent living within you. Having ego thoughts doesn't mean you're a bad person, though. We all can experience self-centered moments that speak to the life challenges we face. The goal, therefore, is to arrest the ego for living rent-free in your mind. You don't have to be steered by its destructive messages about who you ought to be. It's an unfit mechanism to draw logic from. So, it's time to tame it. I'll show you how to catch the ego in action, detach from ego thoughts, and take steps to repurpose ego energy. This way, you can confront ego in the best ways possible.

Spot the Ego

Identify the ego by paying attention to how you think about yourself when you feel fear and self-doubt. You can tell it's the ego because you don't want to be exposed or viewed negatively. Take a moment to point out ego thoughts for a particular situation in your life. Ask yourself, *Could this be the ego at play?* The answer is yes when you notice any of the following:

You change or ditch authentic parts of you. You do this to impress others. Like if you smile a lot by nature. Ego messages can be *Stop smiling so much. They won't take you seriously.* Then you conceal this natural part of you and operate as a less true version of yourself for the sake of gaining acceptance (Kristina 2020).

You feel threatened when there is difference. A person who thinks and acts differently from you feels like a threat to your relevance (Kristina 2020). Or when your approach to life is challenged, you're afraid others will think your ways are weird or outdated. It's like a volunteer who seeks to save her group's documents on an external flash drive. Fellow volunteers tell her, "That's so old-school. Just save it to the cloud." This comment is embarrassing to the person who suggested the use of a flash drive. She feels outed as someone with no technological savvy.

You cast your negative feelings onto others. In your aim to protect your image, you blame others instead of taking responsibility for your own actions. To the ego, accepting blame would mean you are wrong or undeserving. So, you deflect your shame by criticizing others and putting the onus on them (Kristina 2020).

You approach things in an entitled way to feel worthy. Entitlement is a pushback reaction driven by ego. When you're entitled, you're looking to gain privileges to avoid feeling less-than. It's like a stand-up comedian who complains about a particular performer being scheduled to take the stage before him. He worries he'll be outshined by that person. So, he demands to go first. This leaves one to wonder: is the comedian there to contribute to the enjoyment of the audience, or is he there to appease the ego?

CHECKING IN   Which of the four ego manifestations can you relate to the most?

Be Humble

You might mistake imposter anxiety as a mark of a humble person. But self-doubt is not a sign of humility. Humility doesn't involve a lack of confidence. It is, instead, a characteristic of confidence. So don't confuse imposter anxiety with humility. Humility is a healthy understanding of who you are in relation to others. With humility, you don't try to control people's perceptions of you. You're not overly dependent on praise. You're compassionate toward yourself. And you're okay with making mistakes; you don't beat yourself up about them. You're aware of your potential. And you know progress is possible; you look forward to it. Can you see how humility promotes confidence?

But be cautious. In the absence of humility, the ego is present. Unlike humility, the ego is powered by unhealthy beliefs about yourself. Ego prompts you to seek control over people's opinions of you, and it depends on acknowledgment from others to feel valid. When you're led by ego, you judge yourself for your errors instead of seeing the possibilities for growth.

Take a moment to notice ego thoughts when they come, then counter those ideas with humility. You stand to gain a sense of calm and contentment within yourself when you do. To make sure you can point out the differences between ego thoughts and humble thoughts, consider these examples.

Ego thought: *She didn't thank me for cooking dinner. I feel unappreciated.*

Humble thought: *I did my best and I appreciate the effort I put in.*

*   *   *

Ego thought: *I can't influence my team's motivation. I'm no leader after all.*

Humble thought: *If I try to motivate them today and it doesn't work, then I can try a different approach tomorrow.*

*   *   *

Ego thought: *They all dance better than me. I have no business on this team.*

Humble thought: *I look forward to improving. I'm glad I can learn from a squad of super talented dancers.*

CHECKING IN   Make a list of ego thoughts you have that evoke imposter anxiety. Take a few minutes to convert those ego thoughts into humble thoughts.

Use Intuition as Your Guide

You don't have to think long and hard to replace an ego thought with a humble thought, because you have an unmatched resource within you. This support is ever present and ready to help you make decisions when ego thoughts arise. In the Christian faith, many regard this entity as the Holy Spirit. Some people think of it as the God in you or your *inner voice*. Others simply call it a "gut feeling." You may know it as your intuition. This guide gives you a sense of which direction to go. Its messages to you counter ego thoughts. It recommends selfless gestures. It steers you away from fear-based reactions, proposes proactive and wise options, and leads you toward a greater purpose.

You may not get the outcome you want right away when you follow your intuition. If this happens, your intuition tends to give you peace of mind as you wait for the right outcome to manifest at the right time. It's sure to remind you of the sound decisions you make, though, motivating you to continue listening to it when it speaks clearly in your heart.

I learned to pay attention to my intuition. When I face self-doubt, I notice the confidence, certainty, and serenity I gain when I follow the suggestions I gained from my intuition. Unlike the endless rat race of contemplations that ego yields, I can simply attend to my intuitive thoughts and continue forward with my life. My intuition doesn't hoard my mental space. It doesn't take up much of my time either. And because it's never let me down, I intend to always use it as my pilot light. I encourage you to leverage yours, too. Here's how.

First, know ego thoughts can be abrasive in how they come to mind. Intuition is different. Picture your intuition as a soft-spoken, gentle messenger. Because ego thoughts can occupy so much real estate in your mind, you'll have to pause and look beyond them to notice what your intuition is saying. Tap into your intuition simply by asking *How can I apply wisdom here?* The answers you gather from this deliberate inquiry are your guide to letting go of the ego's dominance.

CHECKING IN   Write about how you will embrace the amazing resource you have within you, your intuition. Meditate on all the ways your intuition helps you embrace your best self.

Let It Go

Days before my wedding, I pleaded to Mom, "Please, everything needs to be done on time. No last-minute arrangements." But there's one thing with Nigerians. We are notorious for being late. So, I stood in my gown, with my newly pronounced husband, Kingsley, in the lobby. My parents were supposed to arrive a while ago for our grand entrance. I was pissed. Our grooms-men and bridesmaids were in formation—we were ready to make our appearance into the reception. Twenty minutes went by. Then an hour. Then two! I was fuming. I worried about how the wedding guests would view me. *Will they think my wedding was a flop?* This was *my* wedding. One of the most cherished days of *my* life. It was supposed to be perfect. My anger got so intense, I didn't know what to do with myself. With his big doe eyes, Kingsley said, "It's okay, sweetie. Really, it's fine." You know the saying: "When you hit rock bottom, the only way left is up."

I decided to let my bridezilla rage go. Deep and long, I took a breath and released it. My anger went away fast. Then I started seeing the moment clearly. Gratitude took over. I gazed at my brand-new spouse and remembered how overjoyed I was to be his bride. My wedding party was beautiful. The reception hall reminded me of the day's significance. It was a celebration of love and nothing less. I started to appreciate the magnificence of the moment. I concluded, *They will get here when they get here.* I took off my heels and danced in place with my groom, vibing to the DJ's songs. Our wedding party started moving their bodies, too. A tense environment was transformed into a lighthearted, fun-filled atmosphere. The fear of being judged was no longer a threat to me. I had freed myself.

At last, they arrived, and the wedding procession could begin. When it was time for my parents to walk in, my dad and mom entered, doing their jig. Behind them, in matching baby blue and white outfits, was a showcase I never expected: the largest entourage of women I'd ever seen. They paraded into the hall to a popular Nigerian song and hyped up the crowd. They just kept prancing in—it seemed never-ending. The stunning imagery of solidarity and support is forever etched in my memory. It seamlessly represented the love between Kingsley and me.

The ego told me my wedding was a disaster. But once I released from the ego's grip, my imposter anxiety dissolved. I stopped obsessing about my self-image. I removed my ego-coated blinders; then I was able to see that my wedding was wonderful after all.

You can tell the ego is at work when you worry about people's perceptions of you and you try to control how you're perceived. These are attempts to feel powerful and to protect your reputation, like hiding truths or bottling up who you are. But exerting your energy in these ways creates unnecessary pressure and suffering. Releasing these heavy weights is liberating and empowering. You can run faster, jump higher, be greater. You leave room to focus on what truly serves you. And all of this can be accomplished after you decide to let the ego go.

Repurpose Ego Energy

The ego is toxic when left unchecked. But don't write it off just yet. It's not completely unhelpful. You can gain useful intel from ego thoughts. They reveal what you care about. And if you dig deeper in exploring them, the insights you discover can inform you of something even more significant. Like the greater cause behind what you're doing. Take this scenario of a college advisor as an example. He cares about being impactful in his work. But he's going about it all wrong. He works to be praised for the number of student sessions he has daily. Because to him, meeting with tons of students each day means he's an outstanding professional. He looks for ways to increase the quantity of his sessions with his students, without caring about the quality of his conversations with them. This ego-based approach leaves him frustrated, unsatisfied, and never feeling like he's enough; the applause from his superiors hasn't come.

But what if the advisor repurposed his ego energy? Doing so would help him move beyond his feelings of inadequacy if he, instead, devoted his energies to prioritizing the well-being of his students, aimed for meaningful conversations with them, and eliminated his preoccupation with getting pats on his back. Refocusing his ego energy in these ways is the right solution to his longing for having an impact in his work. By doing so, he gains an enduring sense of confidence and fulfillment from his efforts.

Repurposing ego energy is about spending less time thinking about how other's view you and more time connecting to a higher mission. When you reassign ego energy, you use that fuel to achieve soul-filling goals. The more you use it to concentrate on things outside of yourself, the less insecure you'll feel. You can apply this when it comes to redirecting ego-driven reactions like *entitlement*.

Responsibility over Entitlement

An entitled attitude is when you claim the right to special treatment. So, to feel important, avoid embarrassment, or compensate for the pain of your self-doubts, you require people to favor you. Imposter anxiety produces this pushback behavior. An example of this is from the previous scenario of the comedian who demands to hit the stage before the other performer. His skepticism about in his ability to captivate the audience is what prompts him to seek the unearned privilege of going first.

Behaving in entitled ways is governed by an insecure sense of self. And it's an unhealthy approach for feeling worthy. This hostile reaction also harms your relationships or how people view you. When you're challenged with entitlement and you're looking to repurpose this ego energy, here's what to do. Seek *responsibility* instead. Responsibility is a more effective way to achieve your goals and be impactful in a good way. When you're being responsible, you tap into your strengths to fulfill a cause. People feel more confident in you, and they become more compelled to support and honor you for your efforts. Being responsible is the path to embracing a more secure, healthier version of yourself. Even when you dissect the word "responsible," you see *response-able*, or able to respond, not react. It's the essence of addressing imposter anxiety—to respond effectively. So, there's no need to strong-arm people into esteeming you. Allow your responsible actions to speak for you, instead.

After accepting responsibility, spend time recognizing what matters to you. Use that information to ask yourself, *What's the bigger purpose here?* Each situation may have its own larger objective. Identify and focus on those objectives. You don't have to manipulate how people see you. And you don't have to conform to ego thoughts in any other way. Target the altruistic reasons behind your works, and drive your energies there instead.

A source of inspiration for you could be to view responsibility through a historical lens. Think about your ancestors and reflect on the sacrifices they made so you could experience the opportunities you have now. Bring this awareness with you when you're faced with ego thoughts. It shifts your attention away from your self-image. And it allows you to focus more on furthering a mission you share with the people who came before you. Check out the "Greater Purpose Clarity Hack" in appendix B. This activity will help you gain clarity on the bigger picture behind your efforts and a solid sense of why you do what you do.

> **CHECKING IN**   What greater causes are important for you to remain mindful of? List the meaningful, underlying purposes of your efforts. You can look at this list anytime the ego needs to be checked and your true motivation needs a boost. Use appendix B as your guide.

Emulate a Good Role Model

It helps to identify an exemplar who mirrors what confidence, humility, and responsibility look like. My role model is a political figure who lost races but didn't shrink back and disappear afterward. She held on to her mission of establishing voter rights. When she won office, she kept her focus off herself and her title. And she remained dedicated to the greater purpose of her work. Her efforts were honored an uncountable number of times, receiving what seemed to be endless recognition from all over the planet. Yet she remains humble and purpose driven. Who is your role model? Carry the thought of this person with you and use it to motivate actions you wish to emulate.

You will deal with all sorts of circumstances in life. Many of them will induce ego thoughts. But it's up to you to disarm the ego. Be prepared to spot it in action. Repurpose ego energy, embrace responsibility over entitlement, and model after a good exemplar. You can move beyond imposter anxiety and pursue life more meaningfully when you respond to ego in these ways.

Ego shows up especially in competitive situations. In the next chapter, you'll find out how to respond to imposter anxiety when it's sparked by competition.

CHAPTER 9

Draw Inspiration from Competition

What does competition mean to you? Maybe you understand it as going against an opponent. Or you might view it as an activity you participate in to beat your toughest rival, be at the top of your game, become the highest performer—or be the coolest, the smartest, the sexiest. Competing in these ways is often driven by the ego, but it's fair to note that competing may come with advantages too. Like the times it kept you accountable for finishing a task, motivated you to try your best, or exposed you to ideas of what success can look like after you achieve a goal. Competing may benefit you in some ways, but it can also produce imposter anxiety. Here's what imposter anxiety looks like when it's stirred up by competition:

- You compete to feel greater than others.

- You fear being looked down upon if you lose.

- You judge your value by sizing yourself up against others.

- You feel threatened by someone else's talents.

- You feel tense or isolated because of the friction created between you and others.

- You feel embarrassed or deem yourself less-than if you don't win.

- Learning feels stressful instead of enjoyable.

- You burn yourself out while trying to outdo others.

In your life, does competing trigger imposter anxiety in any of these ways?

You might think back to your earlier years, when you were introduced to competition. Take three-year-old Princeton, who was exposed to competing by his nine-year-old brother Martin.

"Run up the stairs as fast as you can with me," Martin instructed. "On your mark. Get set. Go!"

Princeton saw Martin take off, so he took off, too. Martin reached the top of the stairs first—flailing his arms in the air while springing up and down to celebrate his win. Princeton's eyes were glued on Martin as he watched his big brother rejoice.

"I wiiin! You lose, you lose," Martin sang. This moment taught Princeton that winning is the way to feel strong. To feel secure. To feel worthy. Princeton also learned: if there is a winner, then there is a loser.

Princeton formed a frown, stamped his feet, and wailed in anger. He connected winning with good feelings and losing with bad ones. And with a desire to beat Martin to get that good feeling, he continued to race against his big brother. Running up the stairs, again and again.

In your case, you likely won't find yourself stomping and screaming over a running-race defeat. But in competitive spaces, you may long for what Princeton craved for, to feel capable and worthy. Especially in the areas you feel are important to you. Wanting to matter is valid. It's a common human need. And "losing" seems to threaten that need. We know racing is just for fun. But can you pinpoint the most important characteristic of Martin and Princeton's interaction? Or the aspect of their race that will make them feel warm and fuzzy inside as adults when they think back to that time? The answer is found in Martin's instruction to Princeton when he said, "Run up the stairs with me." The "with me" part is the gem. The boys were together. And *togetherness* is the goal of competition.

It may surprise you to learn that competition is about togetherness. So, to explore this idea more, check out the Latin roots of the word "compete." According to Etymonline.com, *com-* means "with" or "together" and *pet-* means "to fly." When you combine the meanings, you see that to compete is to fly together—to reach great heights as one.

Togetherness unites. It dissolves feelings of isolation. It provides a space where you feel supported, secure, and whole. It instills a sense of belonging. It helps bring out the best version of you. And it creates lasting and tender memories. But if competition is about togetherness, then how did this ideal get lost over time, so much so that competition triggers anxiety and self-doubt?

If you feel pressured to beat others, I can understand why. Especially when competition is a means for survival to attain access and certain resources, like a scholarship or an apartment. Rewards are usually given to those who contend for them. So, you compete to prove your worthiness of those benefits. People also have a natural desire to be liked and to feel competent and important. So, we vie for the *most admired*, *most talented*, and *most valuable* titles. But attempting to outshine others can take its toll on you. It can keep you looping around on a never-ending comparison cycle, where you're constantly measuring yourself up to your rivals.

Don't get me wrong. Comparing yourself to others is understandable, because you could be looking for a point of reference to know if you're on the right track. But picture what your life could be if you compared yourself only to yourself. What would it be like for you to draw inspiration from your rivals instead of feeling threatened by them? And what amazing things could you accomplish if your competitors became your collaborators?

The best way to explore these questions is through Simon and Adam's story. It's an illuminating account of their competition with one another. Through their story, you'll learn about their insecurities as rivals. You'll see how they changed their mindset about their competitiveness to foster togetherness. And you'll learn steps you can take to feel empowered, instead of anxious, by competition.

Story: Simon and Adam

Simon Sinek and Adam Grant are esteemed thought leaders who are internationally recognized for their profound ideas on life, leadership, and career. Simon Sinek is best known for popularizing the concept of starting with "Why?" in a 2009 TED Talk, which has become one of the most watched TED Talks of all time. Then, you have Adam Grant. Adam is the author of multiple *New York Times* bestselling books. He has also been named one of the world's most influential thinkers by Thinkers 50 (2023).

During the 2017 Aspen Ideas Festival, Simon and Adam served as co-guest speakers for the event. Both were interviewed together by journalist Katie Couric. To kick off the talk, Katie invited Simon and Adam to each give opening remarks to usher in the topic of discussion. But their opening statements were more like confessions. Simon spoke first, admitting his insecurities with his rival. He talked about how Adam's strengths are his weaknesses and how Adam's ability to back up his ideas with research findings is what Simon struggles to do. Simon continued, acknowledging his admiration for Adam because Adam's strong suit is not his.

When Adam responded to Simon, he confessed similar sentiments of feeling insecure. Adam described how Simon possesses a charisma on stage that he (Adam) spends too much time trying to build. Simon chuckled, surprised by Adam's admission.

Responding to Competition

Simon and Adam's time at Aspen was the beginning of their public confession about their rivalry. A few years later, the two reconnected for a podcast episode to continue the conversation they started in Aspen. They chatted on Simon's podcast, *A Bit of Optimism*, in 2020. It was a chance for them to deeply dialogue about their rivalry. Much of what they spoke about were lessons they learned from vying with each other. Using their experience as an example, here are six tips to respond to competition the right way.

1. Reject Comparison

For years, Simon would log on to Amazon to compare his book ratings to Adam's. Simon felt bad every time Adam was ranked higher than him. And he revealed that comparing his success to Adam's stirred up his feelings of inadequacy. Do you use other people's success as a metric to judge your own? If so, think about how doing so affects you. Maybe you start thinking, *I'm not that talented.* If you do, then it's time to recognize the harm of comparison and stop using it as a tool to measure your worth.

You might be wondering *How can I know what my strengths are if I don't compare myself to others?* It's okay to observe differences between you and others to identify your strengths. But it's unhelpful to use your differences to *judge* your worth. Let me clarify this. In a quantifiable way, you can have more assets or skills in certain areas than others. Like a billionaire compared to a millionaire. Or a professionally trained dancer versus a new dancer with no training. The billionaire and the experienced dancer have more acquired worth. However, from an existential perspective, every person is equally worthy, because you come with potential, like everyone else. You have human needs, like anyone else. So, no matter how much access, money, or know-how a person has, you are just as important simply because you are alive.

How damaging is it to view yourself as less-than just because your life looks different from others? You have your own time line. Your life doesn't need to mirror everyone else's. In the case where your path happens to look like another person's, your journey still isn't the same as theirs. It could take that person longer to reach a goal than it would take for you to reach it, for example, because all sorts of life circumstances influence how and when things pan out.

You may be the one comparing yourself to others. But consider when people compare you to someone else. Here's how Bethany described her experience as an identical twin:

"If I wasn't a twin, people wouldn't be so bold to constantly compare me to my sister. Growing up, they'd say things like, *She's prettier than you* or *You're the weird twin.* I felt self-conscious anytime I was around my sister at school. She also got way more attention from boys. This made me jealous of her. When people saw me by myself, they'd ask, *Where's your twin?* As if I'm not enough without her. It was a little embarrassing, too. It made me act like someone that I'm not. I wore makeup to be prettier. I tried being extra nice, so people could like me more. And I started spending less time with my sister. Later, though, I realized I missed her. I missed being myself. But mainly, I missed us."

Bethany was her true self around her twin. When they were together, she felt safe and like she belonged. But the influence of her peers had instilled a competitive spirit in her. And it prompted Bethany to pull away from her sister.

Do folks size you up to another person, like Bethany's schoolmates did? Or in what ways do you compare yourself to a rival the way Simon and Adam did with each other? Whether you're the one sizing yourself up to others or someone else is doing the comparing, reject the comparisons. It might feel hard to dismiss other people's judgments of you. But if it's established that everyone is different, then how is it useful to allow comparisons to decide if you matter? You are sufficient and worthy, just as you are.

2. Challenge Yourself

Here's another issue with competing against others. It may require you to move at a speed unfitting to your needs. Imagine what happens when keeping up gets hard and you need a break. How would you feel if you fall behind and get left behind? You may not be mentally, emotionally, or physically available to participate in competition at any given moment. And all sorts of uncontrollable life circumstances can affect the way you show up. There's a healthier way to build your strengths and strive for excellence. This approach doesn't involve competing with others. Instead, it has to do with challenging yourself.

Simon switched his focus from competing with Adam to challenging himself. He spotted the toxic habit of constantly comparing his book scores to Adam's. And when Simon remembered the bigger purpose of his work, he realized how unimportant book rankings were: "The only [person] I had to compete against was myself. I had to make my work better than my work, not my work better than anybody else's work."

Here's what you gain by challenging yourself instead of competing. You get to determine what victory means for you and detach from other people's ideas about winning. You can align your true desires for your life with your own definition of success. And you give yourself permission to work, pause, and rest at your own pace.

Challenging yourself also positions you to focus on deeds over domination. This means you're unconcerned about winning, losing, or being better than anyone else. Your attention is placed on being better than you were yesterday. So, if you're seeking a healthier measure of success, one that doesn't involve competing to beat others, it's found in your efforts to challenge yourself.

Here's how to challenge yourself. Point out what you want to accomplish, then work toward those objectives each day. Take time to reflect on your growth without using other people's wins to critique your own. And participate in activities you're stretched by. You can feel more empowered when you challenge yourself *your* way.

3. Be Inspired by Your Rivals

People you feel are going farther than you don't have to be your competition. Instead, regard them as proof that success is possible. If they can reach their goals, you can, too. Your wins may not look like theirs, but yours are worth celebrating, just like theirs are. Regard your rivals as sources of motivation, and gather knowledge from them. Simon echoed these sentiments when he said, "Rivals are absolutely essential to the growth of ourselves and our work."

To be inspired by your rivals, find out what they sacrificed to get to where they are now. You'll likely learn that their paths weren't always easy to navigate. This knowledge can help you feel connected to them rather than in competition with them.

Cherish the opportunity you have of knowing people who stir your spirit. But I challenge you, take it a step further by telling your rivals how they inspire you. During Simon and Adam's chats, they revealed the qualities they like about each other. Simon expressed how his inclination to compete with Adam ended the day they confessed their insecurities. Which of your rivals could *you* have a conversation with? Think of someone you're involved with at work, school, or in your different social circles—like a person you view as super cool, smart, or skilled.

Once you identify your rival, here's how to respond to your urge to compete with them. Let them know the attributes you appreciate about them. Do you like how they speak? Do you love their ability to organize? Is it their sense of humor? Or are you inspired by what they achieved in a short amount of time? Adam told Simon what he admired about him during the 2017 Aspen Ideas Festival: "There's charisma oozing through the screen. I didn't know that was possible. I remember thinking, *Maybe one day if I get invited to the TED stage, I will be a fraction that engaging and dynamic.*" Telling a rival how they inspire you can ease the friction you might have felt from competing with them. It could also unlock new doors between the two of you in ways you never imagined. So, picture how your openness could strengthen the camaraderie between you and a rival. This newfound togetherness is a good way to dissolve competition-related insecurities.

4. Identify How You Complement Each Other

Your rival may have strengths you wish you had, but you can choose not to focus on what you lack. Instead of envying their qualities, here's what to give attention to: think of their characteristics as *complementary* to your own, like Simon and Adam did. During their chat, each of them pointed out the other one's strengths and acknowledged how their talents are complementary. Adam told Simon: "You have that ability to turn your ideas into stories that people never forget. I desperately need more of both of those things." In response, Simon said, "Our ideas are complementary in so many ways. It's one of the reasons I enjoy your work so much...you add a depth and robustness to my work."

Having complementary qualities with your rivals is a glorious thing. It's like yin and yang—where two entities with different abilities come together to make something seamless. Your yang may look like a competitor or someone you feel outperforms you. But your yang could, instead, be the person you achieve great things with. Here are more cool facts about yin and yang: neither is superior to the other. They are of equal value. They both play meaningful roles in completing a deed. And their relationship ebbs and flows. The yin completes what the yang starts. And other times, the yin begins what the yang finishes. This means the other person can cover you when you need help in one area. And you're there to hold that person up when they need some backing. You don't have to pressure yourself to perform perfectly—you have support from the one who complements you.

The yin and yang blend beautifully when they move together. Like a soprano singing with an alto, fusing their melodies to create a harmony. Both singers contribute their worthy and necessary parts to produce something congruent and undivided. Adam reflected similar sentiments to Simon when he said, "It's almost like we're a whole person when you combine both of our work." Like Simon and Adam, your charge is to identify a *complementor*, someone who holds attributes you admire and who complements your qualities. Who is the yin to your yang? Once you have this individual in mind, think of their strengths as melodies. Then point out your own qualities. They are melodies, too. Are you willing to combine your strengths to produce a beautiful harmony?

5. Collaborate with Your Rivals

People compete to acquire what another person is working to gain. But if you and your complementor have a mutual goal, then why not partner with them to reach it? Like the space rangers in the old cartoon, *Voltron*, a television series about five heroes who defeat big bad villains using Voltron. To construct Voltron, the space rangers link their machine lions together to assemble a giant superpowered robot. Each ranger's lion bot is an essential part of Voltron; if one ranger's lion is missing, then Voltron can't be formed. The rangers successfully defeated the villains when Voltron was activated. But imagine if they didn't come together to deploy Voltron. What if each ranger was alone in taking on the bad guys? Would self-doubt start to creep up and lead each of them to wonder, *Am I able to handle this by myself?* Would a single ranger be as effective in bringing down the villains as they would be when acting as part of a team? Each ranger holds their own set of abilities, but they recognized the power of partnership and combined their forces to achieve their mission.

Collaborate rather than compete. But keep this in mind: a joint effort is more effective when you enter it with people who share your vision and values. It also works better when you trust each other and have established boundaries of respect. Otherwise, you risk entering a partnership prone to unresolvable friction. This conflict could then evoke imposter anxiety, which is exactly what you're aiming to move beyond by collaborating.

Here's an example of this. You have a partner who is careless about time. Despite communicating about your concerns with her punctuality, she continues to show up late without acknowledging her tardiness. You're left to ponder, *Does she think I'm worth being on time for?* From this scenario, you can see how important it is for you and a partner to share the same level of regard for one another.

Continue to explore what you and a rival could achieve together. Could you collaborate for a presentation, meet up to study for a test, or come together to plan a surprise birthday party for a mutual friend? Collaboration with folks who have similar goals presents endless possibilities. It's your chance to be a part of something special. It's an opportunity to receive support and feel assured about your contributions. Unlike competing for the sake of outdoing others, both you and your partner win when you join forces.

6. Enjoy Friendly Competition

Trying to beat others raises unpleasant feelings like jealousy, bitterness, and shame. Simon admitted this when he said, "I didn't enjoy the experience." Because anytime people brought up Adam's name in conversations, it made Simon uncomfortable.

"It was kind of annoying," Adam agreed, as he, too, confessed how he felt when he encountered his own competitive thoughts. But if competition is about togetherness, then why not uphold that positive intention and have *fun* with it? You can treat the experience like a suspenseful movie, where you don't want your fellow watchers to give away what happens in the end. You want to be surprised. Your adrenaline gets going as you anticipate how things will play out, because the conclusion may or may not be what you predicted. This is what makes movie-watching exciting. If you want this same kind of thrill in your life, you can find it in fun and friendly competition.

Friendly competition is an experience of being in community with others in an entertaining way. It can also bring out the best in you. You recognize the strengths both you and your opponent possess. You're also supportive of that person, and you're inspired by what they accomplish. You provide a welcoming space for one another. And because you're comfortable with each other, you might throw in some playful smack-talking. It's okay to encounter a hybrid of emotions during these interactions, too. Like, you might get a little frustrated if you're falling behind. But at the end of the day, you're not using a loss or two to seriously judge yourself. You're just happy about having a great time together. As you can see, competition doesn't have to be a bad thing. It's good when it's congenial and mutually entertaining, because it fosters *belonging*, which is an important source for moving beyond imposter anxiety.

CHECKING IN   You have the power to transform competition into an inspiring and collaborative experience. Reflect on how you can achieve this using these six steps as your guide:

1. *Reject comparison.* What comparisons spark imposter anxiety in you? Ditch those comparisons. Acknowledge your qualities as equally valuable and accept your own unique time line.

2. *Challenge yourself.* What's your plan to step out of your comfort zone to reach goals you set for yourself?

3. *Be inspired by your rivals.* How do your rivals inspire you? Who will you have a conversation with to express how they inspire you?

4. *Identify how you complement each other.* Point out your strengths as well as your rival's qualities.

5. *Collaborate with your rivals.* Think of ways you can join forces to make magic happen. Then invite your complementor to partner with you.

6. *Enjoy healthy competition.* How can you make competition a mutually amusing and welcoming experience?

An Attitude of Togetherness

You learned that the people you think are your competitors can become your complementors. And you can feel belonging when you take on competition in a fun and friendly way. The chance to be inspired, come together, and create a wonderful harmony with others awaits you. So, I challenge you to embrace your new understanding of competition and use it to lean into your best self.

The old ways of competing give rise to the fear of failure. In the next chapter, I'll guide you on how to handle failure. You've likely noticed this concern as a big part of your experience with imposter anxiety.

CHAPTER 10

Turn Failures into Opportunities

As a kid, I relentlessly played Nintendo games with my three sisters. It was a main source of entertainment for us back then. Starting off, I was clueless about how to play. I can recall that distinct jingle. The one indicating that I lost. This tune played every time the clock ran out, when I fell into a black hole or was killed by enemies. I failed countless times. But through those tries, I learned the right buttons to press—I got better at knowing when to push them. And I used the knowledge I gained to progress to more challenging stages. I eventually conquered all the levels and won the entire Super Mario Bros. game. It felt good to finally beat stages I had worked hours to conquer. But the delight didn't come from the wins alone. It also came from the process—the journey of gaming. Studying the dips and turns. Honing my fine motor skills. And exploring exciting new terrains in the fascinating world of Super Mario Bros.

This trial-and-error process exercised my brain. It gave me an experience to look forward to each day. But would my experience have been as meaningful without the failures along the way? Gaming requires you to have quick reflexes, make split-second decisions, use hand-eye coordination, think strategically, apply logic and problem-solving skills, and incorporate teamwork to overcome obstacles—all of which I sharpened through the process and by losing numerous times. I appreciated going through it, because I imagine how empty the experience would have been without my frequent losses. The invaluable chance to build useful skills would have been missing from my childhood.

How about you? Do you embrace opportunities offered through your failures? Even in more serious situations—like a marriage, taking a test, or negotiating a job salary—where you experience losses like a breakup, flunking a test, or getting your negotiation request rejected? You may be left feeling like a failure in these cases. And the fear of being exposed as such is an aspect of the imposter anxiety you face. The fear of failure discourages you from talking about your letdowns. You think if you reveal your failures, others will laugh behind your back. You assume your hardships are points of shame. So, you hold back and suffer in silence. With all these self-limiting thoughts and behaviors sprouting from the fear of failure, you can see why it's important to address it.

But first, let's be sure you're aware of the more constructive meanings of failure. Because failure may or may not be what you think it is.

Failure Is an Advantage

For too long, failure has had a bad reputation. People use it as a reason to shrink, restrict themselves, or avoid going after their heart's desire. But despite any negative views about failure, you can benefit from its many advantages. This is because failure is a good thing. To explain this, I want to distinguish for you what failure is and what it isn't.

Failure is not a person; it's an occurrence. A person who is a failure is someone who can *never* win. So, thinking of yourself as a failure is inaccurate. You can indeed achieve what you want in your life, even after a major setback. This is because you can leverage failure to your advantage. Think about the people in your life who you see as successful or thriving. You look at them and think, *They are winners*. But those who appear to be flourishing have also experienced the biggest failures. What makes them successful is how they *respond* to failure. Naturally, the fear of failing shows up, but they see beyond it. They understand the benefits of failure. And this knowledge empowers them to put themselves out there, take healthy risks, and bet on themselves. Sometimes they win. Sometimes they lose. But their secret is this: they apply takeaways from their losses to drive their wins.

You might think failing is a barrier or a stumbling block. It's not a stumbling block unless you allow it to be. Failing doesn't prevent you from achieving a goal. Your decision to stop going after a goal is what keeps you from reaching it. Even if you fall after a stumble, you haven't failed. Because when you fall, you can still get back up. You can use what you thought was a stumbling block as your stepping-stone—with each stepping-stone elevating you to greater levels. Start by asking yourself, *What have I learned from this failure? How will I leverage my newfound knowledge to achieve what I desire?* When you use your failures to your advantage, your labors will not be in vain. What you thought was a setback is actually your way forward. So, treat your failures like benefits instead of misfortunes.

Can you see, the opposite of winning isn't failure? In many cases, failing is a prerequisite of your success (Burleson and Picard 2004). Giving up on yourself is the true opposite of success. If you're reaching for worthwhile goals, failure could happen at different points throughout your life. Recognize the possibility of this reality. But despite this, your failures don't disqualify you from being, or becoming, the person you want to be.

You may encounter failure as a loss. Like a loss of respect. Loss of relationships. Loss of money. Loss of a good reputation. But with every loss is an opportunity to gain. You gain new chances. You get to cultivate new connections with others. And you get to take the knowledge you gathered from the experience to forge fresh ideas. Failure is not your final stop. It's redirection, moving you toward a more promising and suitable path. So, if failure is rewarding in so many ways, then why spend your energy fearing it?

Failures are an important part of your growth. Without it, you'd be lacking the knowledge, skills, and mindset needed to build confidence and establish lasting success and fulfillment. So, rather than dodging failure, embrace it. You don't have to overprotect yourself to avoid failure. After all, how does it serve you to worry about an outcome you can't fully predict or control? Failure is a natural part of life, and I encourage you to use it to your advantage.

> **CHECKING IN**   Think of a recent setback you experienced. I challenge you to post about it on social media and detail what the experience taught you.

Use this chart to help you recognize truths about failure.

Truths About Failure

Misconceptions of Failure	Truths About Failure
Failure is a *person*.	Failure is an *occurrence*.
Failure is a *stumbling block*.	Failure is a *stepping-stone*.
Failure is a *misfortune*.	Failure is an *advantage*.
Failure is a *missed* opportunity.	Failure is a *learning* opportunity.
Failure is a *loss*.	Failure is a *gain*.
Failure should be *avoided*.	Failure is to be *embraced*.
Failure is *shameful*.	Failure is *inspiring*.
Failure is *final*.	Failure is *redirection*.
Failure is the *opposite* of success.	Failure is an *important part* of sustainable success.

Fear of Failure or Fear of Being Exposed?

Let's unpack what's under the surface of the fear of failure. Could failure as an outcome be the threat? Or is your real concern what others think about you? It's the latter for many. And if it's the same for you, where you fear being exposed as a fraud, think about this. How important are other people's opinions of you? I understand, though, it's natural to want to be loved and respected by others. As social creatures, our longing for connection is in our makeup. However, there's a downside to caring too much about how others view you.

Determining if you're a "winner" according to the outlook of others sparks imposter anxiety. When you do this, it's like you're betraying yourself. You hold people's attitudes to a higher regard than your own. You allow their judgments to hinder your next steps forward. And you stop going after what you desire for yourself. People may define you by your failures and tell you you're not enough. But their attitudes of you don't matter nearly as much as you may think they do. This is because people's opinions of you are just that: their opinions.

Folks are always going to have opinions. And most of the time, what they think about you is based on very little information. People can also be quick to form judgments and use unfair expectations to criticize you. They'll construct beliefs about you even before they meet you. But the people who think you're a failure are often the ones who are the most afraid of being viewed as failures themselves. Can you see how people's perceptions of you don't have any bearing on who you are as a person and what you're capable of doing?

Other people aren't the ones living your life, and they don't have to face the exact situations you face. What matters is how *you* see yourself. So don't fold back because of the way you're perceived. Be willing to view failure differently. And discard other people's negative attitudes about failure.

Set Your Own Standards

In her exquisite red-white-and-blue leotard, Simone Biles, one of the greatest gymnasts of our time, took her position on the floor for the vault competition. It was during the Olympic team finals in Tokyo. The world watched to see what Simone would do to blow us away, yet again, with her record-breaking performances. During her cue-up, many noticed an unusual demeanor. She appeared more stoic than she normally is, with a slightly disconnected look in her eyes. "Maybe she's just being more serious. Maybe it's her new stance," people speculated.

The moment arrived. She blasted off with a sprint. Hit a backflip. Bounced off the apparatus. Twirled her body in the air. And struck a landing, an awkward one. It knocked her off balance to the point she nearly bounced off the mat before catching her fall. Everyone grew still, stunned, and silent. Commentators struggled to find their words. Confusion followed from what the audience had witnessed. Simone's landing was far from what anyone expected. And likely what Simone never intended for herself.

Hours before the finals, Simone had noticed her body shaking and realized she wasn't in the right state of mind. Yet she still showed up and gave it a shot. Simone scurried over to her teammates immediately after and explained her intentions to withdraw from the team competition. Pulling out from the game sent shock waves across the world. Folks criticized her, accusing her of being a "quitter." Some of them blamed her for robbing her crew and her opponents of a chance to compete: "How could the best abandon her team?" they said. Many praised Simone's decision to prioritize her well-being. And the masses appreciated her for sparking a larger conversation around mental health in sports.

Now picture what could have happened if Simone decided to continue with the competition. She reported a case of the *twisties*—a phenomenon where gymnasts feel lost in the air—so continuing would have been too big of a gamble on her safety (International Olympic Committee 2021). She refused to risk serious physical injury for the sake of a game. Otherwise, she would have gone against her values around putting her mental health first. And as much as Simone wanted to participate, she realized this. Compromising herself in that way wasn't worth it. She chose her mental health (Nardino 2022). And rather than stressing herself trying to live up to other people's wants for her, she set her own intentions. When carrying out other people's standards costs you your well-being, stop and question: *What is it worth to me, to endanger myself just so others won't view me as a failure?*

As a reaction of imposter anxiety, the fear of being seen as a failure can prompt you to focus on meeting other people's expectations. You can overcome this people-pleasing gesture by establishing your own standards. You have much to gain by living according to your own wishes. You're free to be yourself. And you have the autonomy to pursue your goals at your own rate. Of course, this doesn't mean you should lower your standards, or only set small goals to make them easier to reach. Doing what is fitting to you is about finding an approach that works for you. An aspect of this method involves challenging yourself to step out of your comfort zone. But as you do this, be sure what you do matches your values and serves your well-being. Aligning your actions with your values keeps you motivated to take healthy risks. You don't have to spend irreplaceable time fulfilling other people's wants. Create your own intentions and see them through. You gain control of your life when you do. You choose what is important to you. And you decide what is good enough for you.

CHECKING IN   Pick a societal expectation you're currently grappling with. Rework that expectation and change it into one that matches your values and what you desire for your life.

Seek Excellence over Perfection

The world celebrates virtues like brilliance and excellence. And our culture bombards us with ideas about being awesome in all we do: *Be a good friend. Be a great parent. Be an outstanding employee. Make a 4.0 GPA.* But these ideals are often misrepresented and abused. If you fail, then your intelligence gets questioned. Or if you make a mistake, then your efforts are disqualified. This is why the old "model minority" stereotype about Asian-Americans is unhelpful, for example, because it puts pressure on this group to perform flawlessly—and it makes them feel less-than if they don't live up to societal expectations. How do you react when you face standards like this? Many carry the burden of perfectionistic cultures on their shoulders and end up developing unhealthy expectations of themselves and those around them. The problem is *perfectionism*—or aiming to make no mistakes—sets imposter anxiety in motion (Cowie et al. 2018).

Are you brilliant? Yes. Because you have the potential to excel in your natural abilities. Being brilliant doesn't cancel the fact that you are human, though. Brilliant doesn't mean perfect. No matter how long you've been studying a subject, and no matter how much you know, undiscovered knowledge is still ahead of you. You can be excellent and brilliant without having all the answers. This is because you have access to innate gifts you can build over time, and by tapping into them, you add value and inspire change in the world.

I challenge you, then, to endeavor to be excellent, not perfect. Being excellent is about doing the best you can with the knowledge and skills you have, without agonizing over what you don't have. It's also about giving your all and not bothering yourself about what you can't control. By replacing perfectionism with excellence, you become more productive—you're not spending your time obsessing over inconsequential details.

Honor Your Progress

Trying to be perfect is often a trauma reaction from being shamed for mistakes in the past. It's based on the false hope of proving you are worthy if you do things flawlessly. If you're one to strive for perfection, your dedication is admirable. And your drive could be what motivates you to pursue greater things in yourself. But at what point will you accept your courageous efforts as enough? Trying to be perfect is like chasing a mirage in the desert. You're never going to catch it, and you'll just end up exhausted and dehydrated. A perfectionistic attitude can also keep you in limbo. You're waiting for the perfect conditions before you make a move. But will that perfect situation ever come?

Use your energy wisely by devoting yourself to your *progress* instead of perfection. Progress is something you can achieve and maintain. You feel a sense of accomplishment each time you reach a new milestone, no matter how small. And as you start to see yourself advance more and more, you'll begin to feel more confident and empowered. The progress you make is excellent in and of itself. So, ditch perfectionism and honor your progress by concentrating on how far you've come.

Trust Your Journey

Trusting your journey can be difficult. Especially when you're constantly bombarded with messages from your surroundings saying you need to achieve certain milestones by a certain age, like getting engaged, married, and with child in your twenties; or purchase your dream home before turning forty. It's easy to get wound up by the pressure to achieve. Because if things don't pan out when we want them to, we believe we've failed.

Trusting the process addresses these fears. This way, you lean into the joys of the journey rather than the stresses of reaching a destination. You believe you are able to accomplish your goals even when you're uncertain about the outcome. You take strides one at a time, even when the process feels tough. And you allow yourself to learn from your mistakes, no matter how severe you think your errors are.

When you assume you're not making any progress and you feel discouraged, remember, the process isn't over. It's a continuous course, starting with a single step. Every accomplishment you're hoping to achieve is built on a foundation of *consistency*. And if you have a setback along the way, be okay with the emotions you might feel, like sadness, disappointment, and frustration. These emotions are valid because you invested your time and energy to reach your goal. So, give yourself a chance to process your feelings. And soon after you do, grab hold of the knowledge you gained about the real meaning of failing. This will embolden you to stay the course, maintain your optimism, and treat your journey as a process worth taking.

Value Your Efforts, Not Just the Outcome

Imagine this. You put in the hours. You stay up late. You give it your all. But despite your best efforts, you don't get the outcome you want. You think, *Was my hard work all for nothing?* In these moments, it's easy to feel like a failure. But are your efforts only valuable when you meet an expectation? What if you viewed your efforts the same way you do when you accomplish your desired outcomes? And rather than regarding your final results as the only measure of success, you treat your efforts as indicators of success, too?

Let me clarify what I mean by efforts and outcome. When you're starting a new endeavor—like building a business, training for a marathon, or learning a new skill—your *efforts* are the actions you take to achieve a goal. They include your routine practices, the time you spend preparing, your productivity habits, your executed plans, and your heartfelt attempts. Think of the different experiences you go through. They are made up of your efforts. As for *outcomes*, these are your results, or your destination. People tend to label their outcomes as a success or failure. But success and failure aren't just results. They are also journeys. They are part of an ongoing process.

As you've learned, your efforts are the motions you take to reach your desired outcome. Does it make sense then, to fixate on just the result without acknowledging the time, energy, and courage you put in? And look at what you accomplish through your efforts. You boldly step out of your comfort zone. And your willingness to try is a testament to your character. Your efforts expose you to new knowledge. You learn about yourself. And you piece together ideas for your next feat. So, value your efforts, flaws and all. The lessons you gain from them are essential to your capacity to push past the fear of failure.

Celebrate Your Failures

As a society, we're not particularly fond of applauding our failures. We're more inclined to hail victories and hide losses. But your triumphs aren't the only events to rejoice over. Your failures are worth celebrating, too. Because every great achievement requires an overcoming of obstacles. And these obstacles often take the form of failures. Here's my encouragement to you the next time you're faced with unmet expectations: delight in what you discovered, how you've grown, and the relationships you built through those experiences. You don't have to conceal your failures. Share about them. Talk about or write about them. When you're open about your errors and setbacks, you demonstrate your appreciation for what your experiences have taught you. You'll also likely inspire a person or two when you do.

> **CHECKING IN**   Write a love letter to failure. You can title it "An Ode to Failure" if you like.

Staying Committed

The fear of failure is a common reason why people give up on their goals or don't pursue them at all. But like Simone Biles, if you find that your path is no longer in sync with your values, then it's okay to quit. Quitting for these reasons doesn't make you a failure. In the case where your goals still match your values—they've been difficult to attain, but you really want to achieve them—I encourage you to stay the course. It's tempting to throw in the towel when you run into difficulties and self-doubt. But the truth is, staying committed to your goals is how to reach them.

Keep this in mind: To move beyond imposter anxiety, remember that failure is temporary. Turn your failures into opportunities. Set your own standards of success. Honor your progress. Strive for excellence instead of perfection. Trust your journey. Value your efforts, not just your desired outcomes. Celebrate your failures the same way you relish in your wins. And remain consistent in achieving the life you desire.

An important resource you'll need to support you through failure is relationships. In the next chapter, I'll show you how to connect with encouraging supporters and use your network as a means for moving beyond imposter anxiety.

CHAPTER 11

Connect with Encouraging Supporters

Imposter anxiety can have you feeling defeated and alone. One viral clip illustrates this, where basketball player Moses Brown lost possession of the ball during an NCAA game (NBA 2019). Likely embarrassed, Moses hung his head low as he paced the court. Then teammate Jaylen Hands came over to Moses, slapped him a low five, and lifted Moses's chin up. Their team was losing by seventeen points. But they triumphed in the end with a score of 87–84, defeating the opposing team by three points (Bolch 2019). Perhaps Jaylen's uplifting gesture had a positive effect on their win. One thing's for sure: there's no denying the power of encouragers to help you move past moments of fear and self-doubt. In your life, do you have supporters like Jaylen? People who can elevate you, pat you on the shoulder, take your hand, and keep you moving toward your aspirations?

You might recall times when imposter anxiety felt down-casting, like Moses portrayed with his head hanging low. But with support, you can overcome that feeling. I'll explain why support is an important remedy for moving past imposter anxiety in this chapter. You'll learn how to identify your supporters. And I'll guide you on how to establish connections with folks who'll have your back.

Support Is the Secret Sauce

Imposter anxiety not only drives a disconnection from your true self but also is sparked by your disconnection from others. This means you aren't actively engaged with supportive figures, and therefore, you don't have the backing you need to dismiss self-doubt. Even the absolute best of the best needs support from others to do the amazing things they do. As iconic as Beyoncé Giselle Knowles-Carter is as one of the greatest performing artists of our time, she didn't reach the top on her own. One interviewer asked Beyoncé, "Have you realized that all you need is you?" In a pleading manner, Beyoncé responded, "Well, I don't. That's not true. All I need is not me. Because I can't do it by myself."

Mrs. Carter is sharply aware of the value of her support team. They are the folks who give her hands-on assistance, so she can show up courageously and fully to entertain millions of viewers. So, recognize how vital it is to have your own network of support (Duck and Silver 1990). You'll be more eager to seek supportive relationships from the right people once you understand how important they are.

As a human, you are neurologically hardwired for social bonds. But when you aren't linked to folks who can encourage you, insecure feelings arise. A sense of security, however, is activated through your supportive relationships.

Support increases your feeling of belonging. Even a symbol of inclusion can do it. Consider a new student who enters a university community wondering if their identity as a gay person will be accepted. When they see a sign reading "Safe Zone: All Are Welcome Here," imposter anxiety is expelled, and they can feel like they belong. This is the power of support.

Support boosts your assurance. But without it, it's hard to know if you belong or if your efforts resonate with others. It's like being new at your job and needing guidance from your boss. Getting trained would help you know whether you're on the right track. However, your supervisor prioritizes other activities and barely makes time to meet with you. These kinds of situations trigger thoughts like *I should have everything already figured out*, or *I'm such a burden to my boss*.

Being supported keeps you motivated to persevere because you know you're not alone. And you'd worry less about the imposterizing judgments of naysayers—your supporters affirm you and encourage you to embrace who you want to be. When you're isolated and without support, you can over-think things and get stuck in your head. But with their words and gestures, your supporters can snap you out of a self-doubting thought cycle. They are there to observe you from the outside, helping you see things from a differ-ent angle. They bring optimism and positive truths to the forefront, urging you to head in the direction you've dreamt of, despite your fears. When you have support, your challenges won't feel as scary, and your goals won't seem as far-fetched.

Who Are Your Encouragers?

You may or may not have a large network. But even if you do, it doesn't mean you have solid connections with the people in it. Here's how to iden-tify the folks you're truly connected to. They are the people you trust and respect. They are the folks who urge you to expand yourself instead of shrink. They help you come out of your comfort zone to go after the goals you feel scared to pursue. They connect you to resources. You feel backed when you're around them. Safe and welcomed. Seen and heard. Validated and emboldened.

Your encouragers could be your best friend, dear friends, or acquain-tances. They could be an advisor, colleague, church member, family friend, family member, mentor, neighbor, professor, sponsor, supervisor, or volun-teer partner. It's also possible to be encouraged by people you know about, but you may not know personally, like influencers you look up to or public figures who are living out the dreams you want in your life. Who are your encouragers?

CHECKING IN   Name three to five people in your life who provide you with encouragement and support.

Level Up Your Support

Getting help makes you look weak is what the ego may try to convince you of. The opposite is true, though. Your willingness to disregard this ego message and seek support is a courageous act. And courage is a strength. The most successful people constantly seek support. You can too. If you haven't been deliberate about building encouraging relationships, then now is the time. Here's how to establish connections with folks who can support you in moving past imposter anxiety.

Talk About Imposter Anxiety Early

Talking about imposter anxiety is an important step to addressing self-doubt. Admit you're dealing with it. And do this as early as you can. Talking about your feelings of inadequacy opens space to receive support from others. This eases the difficulty of navigating the experience on your own.

During the final days of my master's program, our faculty put us through hours of mock interviews to prepare us for our entry into the job market. I was a ball of angst that day. *Would I say the right things when responding to the interview questions? Would I freeze up?* My heart was thumping and my palms sweaty.

I confided in Jill, one of my cohort members, while we waited in the room next door. "This is so nerve wrecking, Jill! I hope I know what to say."

Jill's response immediately took my fears away. "Remember when we first started, and how much we knew then? We didn't know much in the beginning. But we were still able to make it this far. Now, we know much more than we did before."

I was so grateful to have expressed my fears to Jill in that moment. Her reply was the perspective I needed to enter those mock interviews with less panic and my head held high. Who knew that just a few words from a trusted peer could make all the difference? So, recognize the power of revealing what you feel. This very action could connect you to the encouragement you need to go about your pursuits with greater confidence.

Because self-doubt is such a familiar human phenomenon, the people you tell may, in turn, share their own stories with you. Their revealing of a similar experience helps to normalize what you're facing. The sooner you disclose your insecurities, the better situated you will become in overcoming them. Ideally, you'll want to share about your feelings before you enter an activity or start a process. It's understandable if you're nervous about voicing what you're experiencing. But choose to be transparent anyway. Doing so frees you from grappling with prolonged imposter anxiety.

Communicate Your Goals

Along with sharing about your dealings with self-doubt, also describe your goals to the folks you trust. You help your supporters gain clarity on the type of aid to offer you when you tell them what you're aiming to achieve. They also gain a better sense of how to keep you accountable in reaching your goals. When others are aware of what you're aspiring for, they can remind you of the intentions you set out for yourself. They can also be on the lookout for opportunities for you and connect you to resources and other folks who could assist you in accomplishing your dreams.

I used to compete in pageants in my early twenties. Eight of them in total. By the end of my seventh competition, it finally dawned on me, *You need supporters to win.* I'm talking about lots of crowd support. Family and friends who come out with bells and whistles to get you to your victory. I had everything else in place. I had a killer modeling walk. Great presence. Scored high in the interview categories. But I needed a physical representation of support. That was the missing piece.

So, I strategized. I tapped into my network. I told my goals to everyone who said they would come, and I let them know what to do. "I want to win this pageant, so make signs and hold them high. Bring the most rambunctious objects you can find. And whenever the hosts announce my name, unleash the wildest shouts and cheers your insides can muster."

And so they did. Clanking noisemakers and loud ovations filled the auditorium, influencing the judges to view me through an even more favorable lens. I'm sure they thought, *With such a large crowd, she must be worthy,* leaving them with no choice but to honor the audience's wishes. When I walked to the front of the stage and crouched down to accept my crown and sash, I beamed over at my supporters, waving at them, blowing kisses, and mouthing *Thank you.* I did the personal work to reach my goal for the pageant. But it was my supporters who helped secure the win for me. Their support also boosted the confidence I felt during and after the event.

Your supporters can help bring your vision to life. Their presence can give you the push you need to boldly reach for the moon. Communicate your goals to them. You never know how they can show up for you until you give them a chance to. All you need is a bit of courage to tell them your plans, so they can be there for you.

> **CHECKING IN**   Write down one to two goals you want your supporters to help you with.

Name Your Needs

Ask for help from people who can support you. But before you do, think about the different types of support you need. Would a phone call once a month be helpful? How about text messages for a weekly check-in? Be clear on what support looks like for you. Think of support in three ways: emotional, hands-on, or informational (Ko, Wang, and Xu 2013). *Emotional* support can be a conversation to keep you accountable, or it can include words of encouragement. *Hands-on* support involves the physical presence of your supporters, with them aiding you in a practical way, like my pageant attendees. And support can be *informational*, like receiving solicited advice or feedback, where your supporters share their knowledge with you, telling you about their own lived experiences or offering you helpful suggestions.

CHECKING IN   Write about how your supporters can provide you with emotional support, hands-on support, and informational support.

Connect with a Community

Your belonging needs can be met through community. It's the reason people join fraternities, sororities, or other clubs and organizations. It's the purpose for participating in affinity groups. And for many, it's the motive behind going to church. Engage with a group that can champion your personal goals. A circle of supporters helps affirm your worthiness and belonging. So, make ongoing efforts to nurture your relationships in the communities you're involved in.

CHECKING IN   Which community are you curious about being a part of? What can you do to join?

Initiate New Connections

Apart from the people you know, there may be folks you wish to receive guidance or encouragement from. You believe they would make great supporters, so what's stopping you from reaching out to them? If they're famous, it'll be hard to access them. But, for others within your reach, introduce yourself. Get to know them, and allow them to get to know you. As you build trust over time, be willing to share about your aspirations and some of the self-doubting thoughts you're working through.

Request Advocacy

Although asking for help is an effective gesture for gaining support, there's an even bigger game changer if you take your request one step further. This involves asking your supporters to become your *advocates*. Advocates don't just support you with words and tips. The type of advocacy I'm referring to is the kind where your advocates take *initiative* on your behalf. They rave about you in your absence. They're often on the lookout for ways to help you achieve your goals. And they connect you to opportunities they know you'd appreciate, even when you don't ask. Imagine how you'd feel if you knew someone had your back in these ways. Would you feel an increased sense of security and self-value?

To ask someone to advocate for you, here's what to do. Be sure you've established a relationship with them first. Explain how you'd like to see your relationship blossom, so they can feel comfortable advocating for you. Once a mutual understanding has been founded between you and the other person, tell them what you hope to accomplish with their support. And be crystal clear in describing your vision and how they can help you. Being advocated for is a strong source of support. As for your advocates, they stand to gain a sense of fulfillment by contributing to your well-being, growth, and success.

CHECKING IN   Among your supporters, which of them will you reach out to for next-level support or advocacy?

Invest in a Life Coach

You're gaining important mind-shift insights and action steps to move beyond imposter anxiety. But if you're interested in more hands-on support in addressing your insecurities, consider partnering with a credentialed coach. Loved ones can provide great support, but you might need more laser-focused attention from a trained professional.

These supportive figures hold many titles: life coach, leadership coach, executive coach, growth coach, and so on. A coach is a great supporter for maintaining accountability and empowering you to be who you want to be. People generally find great success in working with coaches. And you can, too.

Here's how these partnerships work: A coach meets with you, virtually or in person, to help you uncover any hidden challenges your feelings of inadequacy or unbelonging are triggered by. Through this collaborative process, you and your coach create a specific action plan for responding effectively to fear and self-doubt (Hutchins, Penney, and Sublett 2018). Coaches are skilled at helping you harness your potential and pursue your goals with greater assurance. So, if you're committed to actualizing your aspirations, connecting with a coach may be an important next step.

Your Supportive Environment

From chapter 4, you learned how influential your environment is in your experiences with imposter anxiety, with oppressive spaces being imposterizing and supportive settings being empowering. Picture the life of pet turtles as an example. Look at how much these creatures' environments matter. You could purchase a two-inch baby turtle from the pet store and assume it needs a small tank to live in. After all, it's a tiny creature, right? But did you know turtles grow as big as their environment allows? Putting them in a small tank stunts their growth (Sarah 2022). They'll become unhealthy in such restrictive surroundings. But if you set the turtle up in a larger aquarium, you give it space to expand and flourish larger than you ever imagined. The bigger environment is nurturing to turtles and supportive of their development.

You are like that turtle. Your ability to surmount imposter anxiety depends on how supportive your environment is. So, if you're serious about cultivating a constructive environment for yourself, link up with the right supporters to establish this. Start by identifying who they are, talk about your imposter anxiety feelings early, ask for help, communicate your goals, name your needs, connect with a community, request advocacy, and solicit support from a coach. As you make these strides, you'll discover just how mighty of a solution support is for surmounting fear and self-doubt.

You'll seek support from encouragers to empower you. But what if I told you that being a supporter to others could also help you overcome feelings of inadequacy? In the next chapter, I'll show you how to move beyond imposter anxiety by empowering others.

CHAPTER 12

Empower Yourself by Empowering Others

I wrote this book to empower you. To equip you with the knowledge and strategies to embrace your worthy and capable self. But throughout the writing process, I also ended up encouraging myself. I felt inspired by the helpful knowledge in this book and driven to practice what I preach. The experience also strengthened my sense of self-efficacy. And it has motivated me to be more courageous in pursuit of my biggest ambitions. This is because empowering others is a great way to address imposter anxiety.

By empowering others, you empower yourself, too (Becker 2023). You plant promising seeds through your deeds, lending your words, time, energy, and resources to help others embrace their potential. By sowing these seeds in others, you sow them in yourself. Research has found that service to others is a confidence-building activity (Johnson et. al 1998). A form of service is to empower people through your support and encouragement. So, in this chapter, I'll show you how to use the empowerment of others to move beyond your own self-doubts and insecurities.

What It Means to Empower

Look at the word "empower." When you break it down, the prefix *em-* means "to put into." As for the word "power," it speaks for itself. Put *em-* and *-power* together, you get "to put into power." To empower is to situate someone or to place them in a position of power. When you empower someone, the strength and influence *within* them is activated, meaning they already have what it takes to get started in reaching their goals, but they may feel power-*less* when imposter anxiety is left to run its course in their mind. Their inner authority may seem lost. But it isn't. It can be recovered. The aim, then, is to help them reclaim it.

Empowering others doesn't just benefit the people you serve. Here's how your acts can offer an advantage to you, too.

By empowering others, you focus on a cause outside of yourself. Your attention is shifted away from your insecurities and is placed on the people you're serving.

Empowering others keeps you accountable to lead by example. When you declare positive truths about others, you hold yourself to carrying out the same ideas you use to uplift them.

Empowering others reminds you that you can reach your goals, too. You witness the people you served accomplish things they didn't think they could do. This motivates you to persevere when self-doubt creeps in—because you realize you, too, can hit your targets, if only you apply the affirmations you give to others to your own situations.

Empowering others helps you realize you have skills. When you see the positive results someone gains because of your support, you demonstrate to yourself that you've got what it takes to influence people's lives in a good way. This increases your confidence in what you're capable of doing.

Empowering others fosters supportive relationships. While you're helping someone, you're also building a trusting relationship with that person. Your connection with them becomes the source of encouragement you turn to when you face your own challenges with self-doubt.

Now you're aware of how empowering others is beneficial to you in overcoming imposter anxiety. But how do you do the work of empowering others? You may have a general idea of what to do to elevate another person, but there are certain strategies involved that are important for you to be aware of.

How to Empower Others

The takeaways you gained from the previous chapters are lessons to use in your own life. But also apply this knowledge in your efforts to support others. There are additional gestures to add to what you've learned so far, and I'll reveal what those are next. To get started, think of someone in your life who is dealing with self-doubt. Be their champion by doing the following.

Be Inclusive

I was the only one without a gift. Twenty of us sat together in a restaurant for an end-of-year lunch, hosted by our department head. At the lunch, each person had received a gift from the department head. Everyone, except for me. The department head came over and whispered, "I have your gift in my office. It's sitting on my desk. First thing when we get back, I'll get it to you." I smiled again, then nodded. I had grown accustomed to her games. I didn't care about her gift. But what I did notice when she pulled her stunt was the feeling of exclusion and not being valued.

Be aware of the emotional harm exclusion can lead to. You can help folks feel like they belong. Achieve this by being inclusive, treating people equitably, and factoring in their unique needs (Clark 2020).

One way is to amplify the voices of the overlooked. If you notice someone being discounted, advocate for them. This is what a past colleague of mine did when he noticed how our boss constantly interrupted me whenever I spoke. I always appreciated my colleague's supportive interventions, because his advocacy motivated me to complete my remarks. "Ijeoma was explaining a point, but I don't think she was finished. I'd like to see if she can continue," my colleague would say. I went from feeling silenced to feeling encouraged to speak again. In your efforts to empower others, give folks the floor to fully express their thoughts, free from interruption.

> **CHECKING IN**   How can you be more thoughtful of others when supporting them?

Foster Representation

A girlfriend of mine hosts brunches with a few of her friends, including me. In the group, all are married women with children. Except for one. Dionne is single and without kids. Most of the time, our conversations at brunch are about our spouses or our children. But what about Dionne? I imagine what our gatherings must be like for her. I could understand if she feels out of place in the group and if thoughts of unbelonging fill her mind, like *What am I doing here? I'm not like them.* Dionne takes on a listener role most of the time with a smile and a pleasant disposition. But what would it be like for her if there were more single women without kids in our group? Would she feel more empowered to talk about the things going on in her life?

It's easy to carry on with daily activities without thinking about how our actions affect those around us. This is the case when it comes to being inclusive. Because if you're not deliberately being inclusive, then you might be excluding others by accident. Including others is a *conscious* effort; it rarely happens automatically (Grant and DeBerry 2016). So even when you don't mean to leave someone out, excluding them could still stir up alienating feelings in them.

I would ask Dionne specific questions about how she was doing, to include her in the conversations. In your circles, here's how you can be mindful of others. Make sure each person's identity is represented as much as possible when you bring folks together. This way, people don't have to feel like the "other" in that space. Make your group diverse enough so folks in it don't feel overwhelmingly outnumbered. People are more inclined to express themselves freely in spaces where others share similarities with them. Although it may be difficult to establish a perfect representation of people in your group, creating as much of a balance as possible can go a long way.

Deepen Conversations

Do you hate small talk? Tons of people do. If you're not one of them, great. But if you are, I can understand why. Because these exchanges can feel empty and uninspiring. And small talk is often done out of routine. Recall times when you were dealing with discouraging feelings, but when you were asked how you were doing, you answered, "Fine, thanks," even though you weren't. You were left, then, to process your feelings by yourself. But in your quest to empower others, turn small talk into meaningful conversation. Ask specific questions to find out how the other person is doing. When your questions are more detailed, you go beyond generic niceties. You also reduce your chances of receiving surface-level replies from the other person. When you learn particulars about the other person's experiences, you become better equipped to provide them with more genuine reassurances. Broad-based chats do little to empower people. But when you deepen your dialogue with folks, you forge a path for them to feel seen. Here are a couple of examples of this distinction:

Generic question: "How's it going?"

Specific question: "How's it going with that big project you've been working on this week?

Generic question: "What's up?"

Specific question: "What has switching locations been like for you?"

> **CHECKING IN** What specific questions can you ask when checking in with the person you want to support?

Ask Powerful Questions

Another approach for diving deeper in your conversations is to ask powerful questions. Powerful questions are transformative. They get people to think beyond their current mindset to tap into what's possible for them. And they can sway a person's actions toward their desires. I'm trained to ask my clients powerful questions as a coach. So, I'd like to share a quick tip you can use to do the same for the people you serve, support, and encourage. Ask open-ended questions more than closed-ended ones. Closed questions elicit yes or no responses, or answers that don't require elaboration. But open-ended questions invite people to be more explorative and explicit in their replies.

Open-ended questions usually begin with "what" or "how." So, to ensure your questions are probing, you can start with one of those words. People are experts of their own lives—the ones you help are capable of formulating solutions to their own concerns. But with your assistance, they can feel more empowered to do so. You guide them in identifying their own answers to their problems when you lead with open-ended questions. Here are some examples of open-ended questions to ask those who communicate their self-doubts with you:

"What's the greatest thing that could happen?"

"What's a way forward?"

"How can you make the most of the situation?"

"What's the next best action to take?"

You don't have to be a coach to know how to ask powerful questions. Just remember, this approach only requires you to listen attentively and to be open and curious about the life of the person you're supporting. This way, powerful questions can come to mind naturally as you learn more about someone's experience. Here is what's cool about questions asked out of curiosity: neither you nor the other person may know the answers to them. But your questions get that person thinking of their situation in new ways. Questions you ask out of curiosity are usually empowering. Because through your curiosity, you demonstrate your interest in the other person's life, allowing them to feel seen and valued.

Support, Don't Save

Your goal with emboldening others isn't about forcing things to happen. You know the feeling when others try to save or rescue you from yourself, like those times when you tell a loved one about a problem you're having. They immediately jump into fix-it mode and start rattling off with advice you didn't ask for, saying things like

"You should…"

"You need to…"

"I would…"

Remember how frustrating it feels? Because you're not looking for them to fix your concern. You simply want them to *feel* it. To hear you. To get you. Keep this understanding in mind as you support others. And give advice only when someone asks for it. Like with asking empowering questions, you aren't advising or telling another person what to do. Instead, you're helping someone lean into their ability to address their own challenges.

Giving unrequested advice is a reaction to your own fears, stemming from your biases about the other person's issue and how it would make *you* feel. You end up imposing how you would react onto the person you're attempting to support. The best response, though, is to catch yourself when you notice yourself entering problem-solving mode, and be empathetic and begin asking open questions, instead.

CHECKING IN How did you feel when someone tried to save you when all you wanted was to be seen and heard?

Be Validating

Encouragement can be uplifting. But for many, validating their feelings is enough for them. Validating in and of itself is empowering. To be clear, validating others isn't about agreeing with what someone says or telling them what you think they want to hear. It's not about people-pleasing. Rather, validation is simply about *acknowledging* what another person is dealing with. You accept them as they are and tell them their feelings are okay.

And refrain from judging their circumstances. I admit, it's not easy to do. Because validating someone's feelings requires you to set aside your own insecurities and personal opinions. Pursue the act of validating someone else's self-doubting feelings, after you accept it as a gesture all people deserve. To give you a clear guide on how to validate, here are five actions you can take.

1. Normalize their experience. If the other person shares about their insecurities, let them know, "You aren't alone in dealing with these feelings." Tell them that their feelings are normal. Acknowledge their plight by expressing "I see how difficult this must be." And mention how you can understand their challenges.

2. Share about your own experiences with imposter anxiety. Telling your story can validate the other person's feelings. If you talk about what you're doing to move past imposter anxiety, present it as what works for *you* without sharing it as unsolicited advice for the other person to apply. Be careful not to occupy most of the space talking about yourself. Be brief so you can refocus on the other person.

3. Acknowledge their strengths and efforts. As the person looking from the outside in, point out the good qualities you see in the other person. Remind them of how amazing they are. And shine a spotlight on their progress. Sometimes, people just need help moving the cloud of doubt blocking their vision.

4. Express how you value who they are. It's great to tell someone how much you value them. Say things like "I appreciate you just the way you are." It's even greater to show them, for example, recommending them to participate in something they'd enjoy. You could say something like "Can I connect you to this opportunity? I think you'd be so great for it." Putting your words to action is a powerful way to provide proactive support.

5. Be optimistic about what they can achieve. Express what you believe the other person is capable of accomplishing. Do so by making hope-filled comments like "I believe in you." Be sure to avoid toxic positivity as you do this, though. Because toxic positivity inflicts emotional harm. In *Toxic Positivity*, Whitney Goodman (2022) describes these expressions as statements a person uses to deny another person's negative emotions. These kinds of comments tend to embarrass those on the receiving end and pressure them to suppress their negative feelings. Because of this, they end up feeling unheard, misunderstood, and dismissed.

How to Avoid Toxic Positivity

Toxic positivity can leave you feeling powerless when someone projects it on to you. This happened to me as I stood by the register while the cashier scanned my items. I stared off into space while waiting patiently. My eyes were directed toward the walkway when a random guy marched across it. His bulging eyes met mine when he passed me. And in what felt like a split second after our eyes locked, he unleashed his attacking words. "Smile! It's gonna be all right!" The words he used may seem positive, but his tone was hostile. His facial expression was stern. And his comment was unwarranted.

He appeared appalled as he shot those directives my way. But before I could even snap out of my subtle shock, he picked up the pace and disappeared. The woman who trekked behind him witnessed the berating. Then she softly turned her head toward my direction with her mouth slightly open, just as stunned as I was. The cashier said nothing, but she peered at me with a look that seemed to ask, *Are you okay?* Apart from being told to smile, here's what toxic positivity also sounds like:

"Don't be so negative."

"Be positive."

"Just get over it."

"Others have it way worse than you."

"Crying won't help the situation."

"Be strong."

No matter the types of feelings someone expresses to you, acknowledge what they share. Ditch toxic positivity and make optimistic assertions like these:

"It's okay to let it out."

"Take your time. I am with you."

"I'm here to support you."

CHECKING IN How did you feel when someone imposed their toxic positivity onto you?

Show Open Body Language

When I met Regina, she wore one of the biggest smiles I'd ever seen. Without hesitation, she stretched her arms wide and enveloped me in them. People in college hugged a lot. This was usual. But the hug from Regina was different. Her hug was tight, and it made a strong impression. *Why was she so willing to hug a stranger this way?* Receiving this snug hug from her made me feel worthy. Regina is likely unaware of the impact of her hug. But it's one encounter I will always remember. Because through her warm gesture, I felt safe and willing to be the real me around her. This is the power of unspoken expressions.

Nonverbal gestures are oftentimes more potent than words (Lawrence 2017). So, I invite you to leverage your nonverbal communication. Through your motions, suggest to others, *You are welcome and accepted.* Consider these nonverbal forms of communication:

- *Tone of voice.* Speak in a friendly tone.

- *Proximity.* Communicate warmth with the way you use space when you're around the other person. Practice motions like leaning in or standing close to them but with enough personal space.

- *Physical contact.* A couple of pats on the upper back or a hand-shake can be welcoming. But know the boundaries of the person you're interacting with. Not everyone wants to be touched.

- *Eye contact.* While listening actively, you don't have to stare. But maintain some degree of eye contact in your conversations. You convey, *You've got my attention,* when you do this.

- *Body movement.* Be mindful of what your body is portraying. For example, when someone is speaking to you, do you have your arms crossed? Is your leg bouncing up and down while you're sitting? Is your posture closed off? And do your facial expressions align with what you're saying? Think of the messages these gestures send to the other person. To be empowering, keep an open stance and make sure your facial expressions match your supportive words. Your overall disposition and body movement attests to your attentiveness toward the other person and your willingness to be around them.

CHECKING IN   Which of these nonverbal forms of communication do you intend to express to those you want to support?

Empowering others keeps you accountable to walking the talk. Along your journey, remember to dive deeper in your conversations. Do so by asking open-ended and specific questions. Aim to support, not save. Validate the feelings of those you're encouraging. Be inclusive. Cultivate spaces of belonging. And leverage your nonverbal expressions. You now have the tools to overcome imposter anxiety by helping others move past similar challenges. So go forth and empower the masses. You become a champion to yourself when you do.

Conclusion

You've reached the final parts of this book. And I'm thrilled for you! Your understanding of imposter anxiety should be as sharp as a laser. You can recognize what the experience looks like. You can identify its triggers. You've gained the knowledge to make the necessary mindset shifts. And you're equipped with action steps to move beyond this experience. Let's do a quick review of the key takeaways from each chapter.

Imposter anxiety, an experience of fear and self-doubt, is a *normal* reaction. It can happen at different junctures in your life, especially when you embark upon new or challenging ventures.

There is nothing wrong with you if you experience imposter anxiety. It's not your fault. Outside influences like *oppressive environments* are underlying contributors of this reaction.

Overcoming imposter anxiety isn't about never having the experience again. Expect to face it throughout life as you enter unfamiliar terrains. Although the *inner disrupter* shows up outside of your will, you don't have to succumb to it. The key is to respond to it effectively.

The inner disrupter presents inaccurate notions about who you are. But view its disruption as a sign of success. Its presence is an indicator of your emergence into capacity-expanding opportunities, stretching you outside of your comfort zone. Beyond the familiar is where meaningful growth happens. So, handle the inner disrupter with compassion. Tell the inner disrupter, *Thank you, but I'm choosing to move forward.* And do the opposite of what it suggests.

Unaddressed emotional wounds from past traumas don't just go away with time. So, begin the journey of healing from your hurts, so they don't continue to give rise to imposter anxiety. Reject negative narratives about yourself. Learn about your good attributes, like your personality, experiences, talents, gifts, and interests. Accept positive feedback from others. Affirm yourself. And keep a success document to archive your accomplishments and qualities.

It's a gift to be new at something or to have little experience in it. This state allows you to be present and curious to explore and learn. Your *presence* is power. Focus on your presence over your performance. There is no need to apologize for what you don't know. Instead, replace apologies with empathy, gratitude, and optimism. Acknowledge where you are on your growth trajectory. And honor the progress you've made.

Your *difference* is not a deficiency. It's your advantage. It's your unique edge, not a point of shame. Your difference is necessary, important, and valuable. So, delight in your unique qualities. Use them to create, innovate, and fulfill your life's purpose.

Imposter anxiety isn't grounded in humility. Instead, it's rooted in *ego*. So, identify when the ego is at play. Repurpose ego energy by focusing on the greater cause behind your efforts.

Competition is about togetherness. It's your chance to draw inspiration from others and join forces with them.

Failure is opportunity. Use the lessons you learn from failures as building blocks to reach your goals. Doing so makes your efforts just as worthwhile as your desired outcomes. So, trust your personal journey. Pursue excellence, not perfection, along the way.

You may have all the knowledge to inspire yourself, but *support* from others could be the piece you're missing to lean into your goals. So, level up your support by nurturing encouraging relationships. Talk to trusted folks early about your dealings with self-doubt. Tell them your goals. Name what you need from them. Join a community. Request advocacy. And consider investing in a coach for guided support.

Empower yourself by *empowering others*. To empower is to support and encourage. And to achieve this, be inclusive. Foster representation. Deepen your conversations with specific and open-ended questions. And exhibit positive body language in your interactions with those you're looking to elevate. Aim to support others, not save them. And show empathy for people's expressed feelings without injecting toxic positivity.

Next Steps

After reading this book, how about paying it forward? I encourage you to buy this book for someone who would benefit greatly from this wisdom. Also, I invite you to look for next-level opportunities to achieve your full potential. Your efforts ultimately become important contributions toward a better, more thriving world.

As we conclude, think of the new vision you have for your life. What do you see, now that you have the tools to move beyond imposter anxiety? And what ambitions are you looking forward to going after? The choice is yours. Will you shrink back and allow imposter anxiety to direct your life? Or will you choose to reclaim your personal power and be the architect of your own destiny? I'm excited for you to take charge of your experiences, expand yourself, explore your curiosities, communicate your ideas, occupy space, take risks, put yourself out there, and participate fully. You are well equipped to reach for your greatest aspirations. As you forge ahead, always remember, you are worthy and capable beyond measure.

Acknowledgments

I was able to produce this book with the support of several people. I extend my heartfelt thanks to:

My family and friends for always asking, "How's your book going?" You all kept me on my toes to complete it. To all the leaders, practitioners, and researchers whose work informed this body of work, thank you. I appreciate the folks whose stories were told throughout this book. To Lauren Elliott-Moss, Ken Liddle, and Camille Wilson, thank you for being my beta readers. You donated your time and energy to read the very first manuscript draft and offer constructive feedback. Kudos and thanks to you three. I am grateful to New Harbinger Publications, for taking a chance on me. Georgia Kolias, my acquisitions editor, I am deeply grateful to you for seeing something in me. You were a hard-core advocate to get me on board as a New Harbinger author. And I've learned so much about writing from you. So big thanks to you. To my children, Adanna, Martin, and Princeton, I appreciate each of you for your patience in letting mommy get this book done. To Kingsley Nwaogu, my life partner, thank you for your ongoing optimism and support. You know firsthand how challenging it was to complete this book. And you encouraged me through the hardships. Finally, to my Creator. It was by your grace that I was able to produce a book that is sure to impact positive change. I am honored and grateful to be chosen for this work.

Imposter Anxiety Detox

Here are a series of affirmations. These statements are meant to focus your mind on your capable and worthy self. Read each assertion silently or out loud. As you zero in on the affirmations, pause for a moment between statements to allow each message to settle in your mind before reading the next. Picture what each affirmation means to you. Then reflect on why each statement is true for you.

Feel free to write this out in your journal. Complete this exercise in solitude or with a group. You can download a guided audio meditation version of this for free at http://www.newharbinger.com/51086.

To begin, take a few deep breaths. I invite you to engage your mind and connect your heart to these affirmations.

1. I am worthy.

2. I am necessary.

3. I can achieve my highest and truest self.

4. I am possible.

5. I am more than enough.

6. I don't have to be loud to have an impact.

7. My vulnerability is my power.

8. I will raise my hand.

9. I will speak up.

10. I will be self-compassionate.

11. I will accept my setbacks as learning opportunities.

12. My mistakes strengthen me.

13. I am a lifelong learner.

14. I will trust my growth journey.

15. I will not compromise my values to please others.

16. I will embrace humility.

17. I will focus on the greater good, not the ego.

18. I will take ownership of my experiences.

19. Societal norms and expectations will not inform what I think of myself.

20. When I feel afraid, I will pursue my goals anyway.

21. My ambitions direct me, not my insecurities.

22. My vision is valuable.

23. My perspectives are valid.

24. My dreams can become my reality.

25. My passions are important.

26. I have so much to offer.

27. I have a powerful story to tell.

28. I belong in spaces I'm committed to.

29. I deserve love, fulfillment, and success.

30. My differences make me great.

31. I will boldly embrace my unique qualities.

32. I will trust my intuition.

33. I will not hold back.

34. I will take healthy risks and step out of my comfort zone.

35. I will be an active participant.

36. I will be true to myself.

37. I will reject self-doubting thoughts.

38. I can impact positive change.

39. I will communicate about my dealings with imposter anxiety.

40. I will accept compliments from others.

41. I will affirm myself.

42. I will stay involved to build my capacities.

43. I will draw inspiration from my peers' strengths, not compete against them.

44. I believe practice makes progress.

45. I will surround myself with supportive people.

46. I will celebrate my efforts, no matter the outcome.

47. My self-worth is not one-dimensional.

48. I will use fear as fuel to go after the life I desire.

49. I will tap into my brilliance.

50. I am extraordinary.

51. I can change the world.

52. I can achieve my wildest dreams.

53. I will not give up on myself.

54. I've got this.

55. I am capable beyond measure.

Take a deep breath, hold, and release. I encourage you to revisit this exercise when you're seeking to reaffirm yourself.

You are an overcomer.

Greater Purpose
Clarity Hack

This activity, adapted from "The Five Whys Technique" (Serrat 2017), is designed to help you get clear on why you do what you do. Pick a situation where you experience imposter anxiety. Think of the self-doubting thought or feeling you experience at that time, then write it down.

Once you do this, you will begin the process of asking yourself a series of *why* questions. You'll do this about four to six times: each follow-up question will be informed by your previous answer. For the first why question, write the immediate answer that comes to mind. Be completely honest with yourself, no matter how egotistical your answer may sound. Continue along in asking *Why?*

Once you've completed the activity, reflect on your responses. You may find that your first few answers are ego driven. But as you move closer to your final answer, you'll see that your responses become less egocentric and more big picture. You know you've identified the greater purpose of your work when your final answer is not solely about you. Here's an example of what the process looks like:

The self-doubting thought or feeling:

I'm scared to speak in class.

Why do you feel scared to speak in class?

Because I want to be seen as smart.

Why do you want to be seen as smart?

Because I want to feel good about myself.

Why do you want to feel good about yourself?

Because I want to be happy and content.

Why do you want to be happy and content?

Because I want to feel motivated to be productive.

Why do you want to be productive?

Because I desire to be useful in society.

Why do you desire to be useful in society?

Because I want to make the world a better place.

Examine the final answer. Pay attention to the part that reads, "make the world a better place." That's the big picture. That's the larger objective.

You can imagine how focusing on making the world a better place shifts your energy. In this example, keeping the big picture motive at the forefront empowers you to speak up in class. You become more actively involved, learning as much as you can, so you can apply your knowledge to make the world better. And you feel responsible for adding to the learning of your peers so they, too, can be impactful in society. Getting clear on why you do what you do helps you bypass self-sabotaging behaviors and show up as your best self.

You now know how to identify the bigger reasons behind your actions. It's your turn to try it. For a downloadable worksheet, visit http://www.new harbinger.com/51086.

References

ABC News. 2017. "Oscar-Winning Actress Viola Davis Says She Struggles with 'Impostor Syndrome,'" February 28. https://abcnews.go.com/Entertainment/oscar-winning-actress-viola-davis-struggles-impostor-syndrome/story?id=45789758.

Ahlfeld, A. 2009. "The Imposter Phenomenon Revisited: The Intersection of Race, Gender, and Professional Status for Women of Color." *Dissertation Abstracts International* 70 (9–B): 5803.

Allen, M. 2021. "MasterChef Winner Christine Ha Dishes on Being the First Blind Contestant—Exclusive Interview." *Mashed*, August 6. https://www.mashed.com/479924/masterchef-winner-christine-ha-dishes-on-being-the-first-blind-contestant-exclusive-interview.

Barry, S. 2020. "This Is Why 50 Percent of Multicultural Women Are Thinking About Leaving Their Jobs in the Next Two Years." *MSNBC Business Culture*, July 23. https://www.msnbc.com/know-your-value/why-50-multicultural-women-are-thinking-about-leaving-their-jobs-n1234734.

Bastian, R. 2019. "Why Imposter Syndrome Hits Underrepresented Identities Harder, and How Employers Can Help." *Forbes*, November 26. https://www.forbes.com/sites/rebekahbastian/2019/11/26/why-imposter-syndrome-hits-underrepresented-identities-harder-and-how-employers-can-help/?sh=129dbf1333c1.

Baysu, G., and K. Phalet. 2019. "The Up- and Downside of Dual Identity: Stereotype Threat and Minority Performance." *Journal of Social Issues* 75 (2): 568–91.

Becker, J. 2023. "The Benefit of Helping Others." Becoming Minimalist. https://www.becomingminimalist.com/offer-to-help/.

Bolch, B. 2019. "UCLA's Amazing Rally Against Oregon a Result of Chins, Spirits Held High, Players Say." *Los Angeles Times*, January 11. https://www.latimes.com/sports/ucla/la-sp-ucla-oregon-comeback-20190111-story.html.

Bourdieu, P. 1986. "The Forms of Capital." In *Handbook of Theory and Research for the Sociology of Education*, edited by J. Richardson. Westport, CT: Greenwood.

Bravata, D. M., S. A. Watts, A. L. Keefer, D. K. Madhusudhan, K. T. Taylor, D. M. Clark, R. S. Nelson, K. O. Cokley, and H. K. Hagg. 2020. "Prevalence, Predictors, and Treatment of Impostor Syndrome: A Systematic Review." *Journal of General Internal Medicine* 35 (4): 1252–75.

Brigham Young University. 2012. "Women Speak Less When They're Outnumbered." *ScienceDaily*, September 18. https://www.sciencedaily.com/releases/2012/09/120918121257.htm.

Burey, J. A. 2020. "Why You Should Not Bring Your Authentic Self to Work." TEDxSeattle. https://tedxseattle.com/talks/jodi-ann-burey-why-you-should-not-bring-your-authentic-self-to-work/.

Burleson, W., and R. Picard. 2004. "Affective Agents: Sustaining Motivation to Learn Through Failure and a State of 'Stuck.'" MIT Media Lab, Cambridge, MA.

Canadian Mental Health Association, BC Division. 2015. "Difference Between Anxiety and Anxiety Disorder." Canadian Mental Health Association, BC Division. https://www.heretohelp.bc.ca/q-and-a/whats-the-difference-between-anxiety-and-an-anxiety-disorder#:~:text=Anxiety%20is%20a%20problem%20when,in%20order%20to%20avoid%20anxiety.

Caselman, T. P., P. Self, and A. Self. 2006. "Adolescent Attributes Contributing to the Imposter Phenomenon." *Journal of Adolescence* 29 (3): 395–405.

Cikanavicius, D. 2017. "The Trap of External Validation for Self-Esteem." *PsychCentral*, August 28. https://psychcentral.com/blog/psychology-self/2017/08/validation-self-esteem#1.

Clance, P. R., and S. A. Imes. 1978. "The Imposter Phenomenon in High Achieving Women: Dynamics and Therapeutic Intervention." *Psychotherapy: Theory, Research and Practice* 15 (3): 241–47.

Clark, T. 2020. *The 4 Stages of Psychological Safety*. New York: Berrett-Koehler Publishers.

Cokley, K., G. Awad, L. Smith, S. Jackson, O. Awosogba, A. Hurst, S. Stone, L. Blondeau, and D. Roberts. 2015. "The Roles of Gender Stigma

Consciousness, Impostor Phenomenon and Academic Self-Concept in the Academic Outcomes of Women and Men." *Sex Roles* 73 (9–10): 414–26.

Cowie, M. E., L. J. Nealis, S. B. Sherry, P. L. Hewitt, and G. L. Flett. 2018. "Perfectionism and Academic Difficulties in Graduate Students: Testing Incremental Prediction and Gender Moderation." *Personality and Individual Differences* 123: 223–28.

Croitoru, G., N. V. Florea, C. A. Ionescu, V. O. Robescu, L. Paschia, M. C. Uzlau, and M. D. Manea. 2022. "Diversity in the Workplace for Sustainable Company Development." *Sustainability* 14 (11): 6728.

Cuddy, A. 2015. *Presence: Bringing Your Boldest Self to Your Biggest Challenges.* New York: Little, Brown and Company.

———. 2012. "Your Body Language May Shape Who You Are." TEDGlobal. https://www.ted.com.

Cuddy, A. J. C., C. A. Wilmuth, A. J. Yap, and D. R. Carney. 2015. "Preparatory Power Posing Affects Nonverbal Presence and Job Interview Performance." *Journal of Applied Psychology* 100 (4): 1286–95.

Duck, S., and R. Cohen Silver, eds. 1990. *Personal Relationships and Social Support.* Los Angeles: Sage.

Dunn, J. 2013. "Jennifer Lopez Is Our October Cover Girl!" *Cosmopolitan,* September 3. https://www.cosmopolitan.com/entertainment/celebs /news/a15442/jennifer-lopez-october-2013/.

Flasher, Jack. 1978. "Adultism." *Adolescence* 13 (51): 517–23.

France, P. 2019. "The Value of Vulnerability." *Educational Leadership* 77 (1): 78–82.

Fritson, K. 2008. "Impact of Journaling on Students' Self-Efficacy and Locus of Control." *InSight: A Journal of Scholarly Teaching* 3: 75–83.

Garcia, S. M., T. Avishalom, and T. M. Schiff. 2013. "The Psychology of Competition: A Social Comparison Perspective." *Perspectives on Psychological Science* 8 (6): 634–50.

Gardner, H. 1983. *Frames of Mind: The Theory of Multiple Intelligences.* New York: Basic Books.

Gibson, E. J., and R. D. Walk. 1960. "The 'Visual Cliff.'" *Scientific American* 202 (4): 64–71.

Gildersleeve, R., N. Croom, and P. Vasquez. 2011. "'Am I Going Crazy?!': A Critical Race Analysis of Doctoral Education." *Equity and Excellence in Education* 44 (1): 93–114.

Gillum, A., and R. Jai Gillum. 2020. "Andrew and R. Jai Gillum" interview. By Tamron Hall. *Tamron Hall*, season 2 premiere, September 14. Summerdale Productions. https://tamronhallshow.com/episodes /monday-9-14-20/.

Goodman, R. D. 2015. "A Liberatory Approach to Trauma Counseling: Decolonizing Our Trauma-Informed Practices." In *Decolonizing "Multicultural" Counseling Through Social Justice*, edited by R. D. Goodman and P. C. Gorski. New York: Springer.

Goodman, W. 2022. *Toxic Positivity: Keeping It Real in a World Obsessed with Being Happy*. New York: Penguin Random House.

Grande, T. 2018. "What are Emotions, Feelings, Affect, and Mood?" February 4. https://www.youtube.com/watch?v=55_-YsfSPK0.

Grant, A. 2020. "A Bit of Everything with Adam Grant." *A Bit of Optimism* podcast with Simon Sinek, November 10. https://simonsinek.com /podcast/episodes/a-bit-of-everything-with-adam-grant.

Grant, A., and S. Sinek. 2017. "Aspen Ideas Festival: Why Millennials Work the Way They Do," interview by Katie Couric. MPR News podcast, July 6. https://www.mprnews.org/story/2017/07/06/aspen-ideas -festival-millennials-in-the-workplace.

Grant, H., and J. DeBerry. 2016. "INCLUDE: The Neuroscience of Smarter Teams." *NeuroLeadership Institute*, April 27. https://neuroleadership.com /portfolio-items/preview-include/.

Hanks, T. 2016. "Tom Hanks Says Self-Doubt Is 'A High-Wire Act That We All Walk.'" *Fresh Air* with Terry Gross podcast, April 26. https:// freshairarchive.org/segments/tom-hanks-says-self-doubt-high-wire-act -we-all-walk-0.

Harrison, L. A., C. Ahn, and R. Adolphs. 2015. "Exploring the Structure of Human Defensive Responses from Judgments of Threat Scenarios." *PLoS ONE* 10 (8): e0133682.

Holiday, R. 2016. *Ego Is the Enemy*. New York: Portfolio/Penguin.

Hupp, S. D., D. Reitman, and J. D. Jewell. 2008. "Cognitive-Behavioral Theory." In *Handbook of Clinical Psychology*, edited by M. Hersen and

A. M. Gross. Vol. 2, *Children and Adolescents*. Hoboken, NJ: John Wiley and Sons.

Hutchins, H., L. Penney, and L. Sublett. 2018. "What Imposters Risk at Work: Exploring Imposter Phenomenon, Stress Coping, and Job Outcomes." *Human Resource Development Quarterly* 29 (4): 31–48.

International Olympic Committee. 2021. "What Are the Twisties?" July 27. https://olympics.com/en/news/what-are-the-twisties.

Johnson, M. K., T. Beebe, J. T. Mortimer, and M. Snyder. 1998. "Volunteerism in Adolescence: A Process Perspective." *Journal of Research on Adolescence* 8 (3): 309–32.

Kelly, A. 2010. "Are People Who Act Superior Really Insecure?" *Psychology Today*, November 10. https://www.psychologytoday.com/us/blog/insight/201011/are-people-who-act-superior-really-insecure.

Ko, H. C., L. L. Wang, and Y. T. Xu. 2013. "Understanding the Different Types of Social Support Offered by Audience to A-List Diary-Like and Informative Bloggers." *Cyberpsychology, Behavior, and Social Networking* 16 (3): 194–99.

Kristina, J. 2020. "The Difference Between the Ego Self and Your True Self." December 16. https://www.youtube.com/watch?v=xfrkVMCif9M&t=65s.

Kupperschmidt, B. R. 2006. "Carefronting: Caring Enough to Confront. A Reprint." *The Oklahoma Nurse* 51 (2): 22–23.

Lane, J. 2015. "The Imposter Phenomenon Among Emerging Adults Transitioning into Professional Life: Developing a Grounded Theory." *Adultspan Journal* 14 (2):114–28.

Lawrence, S. 2017. "The Power of Nonverbal Communication." *Integrated Studies* 79. https://digitalcommons.murraystate.edu/bis437/79/.

Licalzi, M., and O. Surucu. 2012. "The Power of Diversity over Large Solution Spaces." *Management Science* 58 (7): 1408–21.

Mobbs, D., C. Hagan, T. Dalgleish, B. Silston, and C. Prévost. 2015. " The Ecology of Human Fear: Survival Optimization and the Nervous System." *Frontiers in Neuroscience* 9: 55. https://www.frontiersin.org/articles/10.3389/fnins.2015.00055/full.

Murphy, M. 2017. *Hiring for Attitude: A Revolutionary Approach to Recruiting and Selecting People with Both Tremendous Skills and Superb Attitude.* New York: McGraw Hill Education.

NBA. 2019. "The Best Videos of NBA and Sports." YouTube. https://youtube
.com/shorts/TVMS7-lgC68?feature=share.

Nardino, M. 2022. "Simone Biles' Most Honest Quotes About Mental Health
and Wellness Through the Years: 'We're Human.'" US Weekly, March 29.

Neubert, J. 2016. "10 Ways Competitions Enhance Learning," July 4.
Institute of Competition Sciences. https://www.competitionsciences.org
/2016/07/04/10-ways-competitions-enhance-learning/.

Obama, M. 2018. "Michelle Obama on the Power of Education and
Self-Belief." Penguin Talks, December 17. Penguin Books UK. https://
www.youtube.com/watch?v=k6KSiZ2KA8s&t=556s.

Phillips, K. 2014. "How Diversity Works." Scientific American 311 (4): 42–47.

Rees, E. 2006. S.H.A.P.E.: Finding and Fulfilling Your Unique Purpose for Life.
Grand Rapids, MI: Zondervan.

Robinson, J. 2018. "Imposterized: The Experiences of Tenured and Tenure-
Track Black Women Instructional Faculty at California Community
Colleges." ProQuest Dissertations Publishing, California State University,
Long Beach.

Ross, D. 2022. "Secrets of Story-Telling with Dennis Ross." The Jake and
Gino Show (podcast), October 20. https://jakeandgino.com/learn-the
-secrets-of-story-telling-with-dennis-ross/.

Ross, R. 2017. "Insecurity Is an Ego Trip We Can Always Come Home From."
Huffpost, March 5. https://www.huffpost.com/entry/insecurity-is-an-ego
-trip-we-can-always-come-home-from_b_58bc601fe4b02eac8876cffc.

Sandberg, S., with N. Scovell. 2013. Lean in: Women, Work, and the Will to
Lead. New York: Alfred A. Knopf.

Sarah. 2022. "Do Turtles Grow to the Size of Their Tank?" Fur, Wings and
Scaly Things (blog). August 24. https://furwingsandscalythings.com/do
-turtles-grow-to-size-of-tank/.

Serrat, O. 2017. "The Five Whys Technique." In Knowledge Solutions.
Springer, Singapore. https://doi.org/10.1007/978-981-10-0983-9_32.

Sinek, S. 2009. "Start with Why: How Great Leaders Inspire Action."
TEDxPugetSound. https://www.ted.com/talks/simon_sinek_how_great
_leaders_inspire_action/comments.

Smith, A. 2019. "Love Your Competitors—How Great Businesses Do Strategy."

TEDxFolkestone, September 20. https://smithesq.medium.com/tedx-talk -love-your-competitors-how-great-businesses-do-strategy-fedfdf19c0ed.

Thinkers 50. 2023. "Adam Grant." Best of Management Thinking. https://thinkers50.com/biographies/adam-grant/.

Thomas, K. M., J. Johnson-Bailey, R. E. Phelps, N. M. Tran, and L. Johnson. 2013. "Women of Color at Midcareer: Going from Pet to Threat." In *Psychological Health of Women of Color: Intersections, Challenges, and Opportunities*, edited by L. Comas-Diaz and B. Greene. Santa Barbara, CA: Praeger.

Thomas, R., M. Cooper, K. M. Urban, G. Cardazone, M. Noble-Tolla, S. Mahajan, B. Edwards, L. Yee, A. Krivkovich, I. Rambachan, W. W. Liu, M. Williams, N. Robinson, and H. Nguyen. 2022. *Women in the Workplace*. Lean In and McKinsey and Company. https://wiw -report.s3.amazonaws.com/Women_in_the_Workplace_2022.pdf.

Tiedens, L. Z., and A. R. Fragale. 2003. "Power Moves: Complementarity in Dominant and Submissive Nonverbal Behavior." *Journal of Personality and Social Psychology* 84 (3): 558–68.

Tulshyan, R., and J. A. Burey. 2021. "Stop Telling Women They Have Imposter Syndrome." *Harvard Business Review*, February 11. https:// hbr.org/2021/02/stop-telling-women-they-have-imposter-syndrome.

Wang, C. 2020. "To Cope with a New Coronavirus Pandemic: How Life May Be Changed Forever." *Chinese Journal of International Law* 19 (2): 221–28.

Williams, K. D., and B. Jarvis. 2006. "Cyberball: A Program for Use in Research on Interpersonal Ostracism and Acceptance." *Behavior Research Methods* 38 (1): 174–180.

Williams, K. D., and S. A. Nida. 2011. "Ostracism: Consequences and Coping." *Current Directions in Psychological Science* 20 (2): 71–75.

World Health Organization. 2022. "Mental Health and COVID-19: Early Evidence of the Pandemic's Impact: Scientific Brief," March 2. World Health Organization. https://www.who.int/publications/i/item/WHO -2019-nCoV-Sci_Brief-Mental_health-2022.1.

Ijeoma C. Nwaogu, PhD, is an accredited coach and owner of Everlead, LLC, a leadership development consulting enterprise. She has captivated audiences nationwide through engaging talks, workshops, and conference sessions focused on empowering individuals to overcome imposter anxiety. With over sixteen years of experience in higher education, Nwaogu has made significant contributions as an educator and administrator. She was a director of the Multicultural Center at Rice University, where she fostered inclusivity and cultural understanding. She served as an adjunct professor at the University of Houston, imparting valuable knowledge and guidance to aspiring professionals. Nwaogu's academic journey includes a doctoral degree in counseling and a master's degree in college student affairs administration, both earned from the University of Georgia. She laid the foundation for her educational pursuits with a bachelor's degree in psychology and sociology from Georgia State University.

Real change *is* possible

For more than forty-five years, New Harbinger has published proven-effective self-help books and pioneering workbooks to help readers of all ages and backgrounds improve mental health and well-being, and achieve lasting personal growth. In addition, our spirituality books offer profound guidance for deepening awareness and cultivating healing, self-discovery, and fulfillment.

Founded by psychologist Matthew McKay and Patrick Fanning, New Harbinger is proud to be an independent, employee-owned company. Our books reflect our core values of integrity, innovation, commitment, sustainability, compassion, and trust. Written by leaders in the field and recommended by therapists worldwide, New Harbinger books are practical, accessible, and provide real tools for real change.

newharbingerpublications

MORE BOOKS from
NEW HARBINGER PUBLICATIONS

**REWIRE YOUR
ANXIOUS BRAIN**

How to Use the Neuroscience
of Fear to End Anxiety,
Panic, and Worry

978-1626251137 / US $18.95

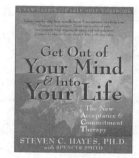

**GET OUT OF YOUR MIND
AND INTO YOUR LIFE**

The New Acceptance and
Commitment Therapy

978-1648483226 / US $24.95

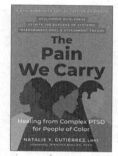

THE PAIN WE CARRY

Healing from Complex PTSD
for People of Color

978-1684039319 / US $17.95

SH*T I SAY TO MYSELF

40 Ways to Ditch the Negative
Self-Talk That's Dragging You Down

978-1684039555 / US $16.95

**THE EMOTIONALLY
EXHAUSTED WOMAN**

Why You're Feeling Depleted
and How to Get What You Need

978-1648480157 / US $18.95

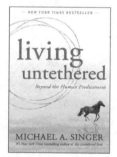

LIVING UNTETHERED

Beyond the Human Predicament

978-1648480935 / US $18.95

Did you know there are **free tools** you can download for this book?

Free tools are things like **worksheets, guided meditation exercises**, and **more** that will help you get the most out of your book.

You can download free tools for this book—whether you bought or borrowed it, in any format, from any source—from the New Harbinger website. All you need is a NewHarbinger.com account. Just use the URL provided in this book to view the free tools that are available for it. Then, click on the "download" button for the free tool you want, and follow the prompts that appear to log in to your NewHarbinger.com account and download the material.

You can also save the free tools for this book to your **Free Tools Library** so you can access them again anytime, just by logging in to your account! Just look for this button on the book's free tools page.

+ Save this to my free tools library

If you need help accessing or downloading free tools, visit **newharbinger.com/faq** or contact us at **customerservice@newharbinger.com**.